YES! TO Love™

The Ultimate Guide to Personal Transformation for Everyday Life Balance

Pascale D. Gibon

Providence Publishing Ltd
London, England

Published by Providence Publishing Ltd
25 Glazbury road
London, W14 9AS
United Kingdom

Yes! To Love™
The Ultimate Guide to Personal Transformation for Everyday Life Balance

ISBN regular Print Edition: 978-0-9935198-0-2
ISBN eBook Edition: 978-0-9935198-1-9

For information about special discounts for bulk purchases, please contact Providence Publishing Ltd.

Printed in the United States of America

Visit us online at: www.yestolovebook.com

Contents

Praise for YES! TO Love™

"Wow! Pascale D. Gibon has produced a remarkable book. Yes! To Love is an effective and practical guide for greater life balance. The 3 steps formula for everyday life balance is easy to follow and will help you transform your life."
Raymond Aaron, New York Times #1 Best-selling Author

"I highly recommend this book to anyone who wishes to learn how to best respond to the challenges of life and thus find greater life balance."
Robert G. Allen, New York Times Best-selling Author

"If you want greater inner peace and balance in your life, Pascale D. Gibon's amazing insight takes you by the hand and guides you toward greater emotional balance and personal effectiveness."
Chris James, Founder of Chris James Mind Body

"I love Pascale D. Gibon's vision for greater inner peace. Saying Yes! To Love changes everything and requires you to look at your life from a new perspective."
Jalal Miah, Author of *HEART Way to Success*™

"I have learned so much from Pascale with regard to improving the quality of my life, building my self-confidence and following my heart."
Kate Picon, London, UK

"Pascale can truly transform your life follow her coaching."
Kay Steele, London, UK

"If you want to experience greater balance in your life, Yes! To Love is the wonderful book that you need. You will not only learn how to find inner peace but also how to live a less stressful and more fulfilling life."
Paulo Tercio, Painter & Photographer

I dedicate this book to my beloved grandmother who taught me humility, love, wit and wisdom.

Note to the Reader

The information, including opinion and analysis, contained herein is based on the author's personal experiences.

The author and the publisher make no warranties, either expressed or implied, concerning the accuracy, applicability, effectiveness, reliability or suitability of the contents. If you wish to apply or follow the advice or recommendations mentioned herein, you take full responsibility for your actions. The author and publisher of this book shall in no event be held liable for any direct, indirect, incidental or consequential damages arising directly or indirectly from the use of any of the information contained in this book.

All content is for information only and is not warranted for content accuracy or any other implied or explicit purpose.

Foreword

In today's modern society people increasingly suffer from high levels of stress and 'overwhelmed syndrome.' In her book *Yes! To Love*™ Pascale D. Gibon raises the following question: what would your life be like if you were to live every day from a place of greater love?

Yes! To Love™ suggests that when you deepen love for yourself, your life, for others and for the world everything changes and your life becomes more balanced. Indeed, Pascale reveals that it is your attitude to life that creates the imbalance, and you will discover in this book what attitude would favour greater balance and daily inner peace.

Pascale also shares easy and practical processes you can implement to create your desired outcome. In particular, the 3 'Ms' formula of everyday life balance™ is a simple formula to follow, which will give you greater clarity.

Personally, I have now included more holidays in my yearly agenda. I go on holiday for one week every month and for two months over the summer. This allows me to spend more time with my loved ones. I made it a priority to become a better husband, a better father and a better teacher. Living a balanced life makes it all worthwhile.

I have known Pascale since 2012 and it is true that each time I meet her she radiates peace and harmony. She imparts her wisdom in her book *Yes! To Love*™.

Should you want to achieve greater balance in your life, this book will inspire you and motivate you to take action and will provide you with practical tools for self-transformation. It is Pascale Gibon's mission to create happiness in the world and it starts simply with your happiness.

I highly recommend that you read this book now and get started on creating greater balance in your life.

Raymond Aaron

New York Times #1 Best-selling Author

Acknowledgments

From the bottom of my heart, I thank God, my beloved family, and friends.

My special thanks to Dr. Asma B Omer who gave me the opportunity to write this book by inviting me, as her guest, to my first book writing workshop.

Special thanks to my mentors, Bob Proctor, Doreen Virtue, Diana Cooper, Carolyn Myss, Les Brown, Michael Neill, Janet Bray-Attwood & Chris Attwood, Deepak Chopra, Wayne Dyer, Robert Kiyosaki, Robert Allen, Marianne Williamson, Lester Levenson, Raymond Aaron, Jack Canfield, Mark Victor Hansen, Chris Gardner and Master Ryuho Okawa for their inspiration, vision and teachings.

My heartfelt thanks to my yoga teacher and friend Chris James.

My heartfelt thanks to my Reiki master, Barbara McGregor, and the Usui Reiki Network for changing my life forever.

My special thanks to Christian Gibon, Marie-Jose Gibon, Monique Telchild, Rosemonde Telchid, Chris James, Anna Di Giovine, Phil Benton, Helena Ambrosio, Paulo Tercio, Sayo Ouchi, Margarita Falagan, Minnie Nabali, Kate Picon, Kay Steele, Aruna & Ravi Ravithasan and Swan Treasure for believing in this book project and for their encouragement. I did it!

My special thanks to my clients, students and to all of the people I have met who have inspired me to make of this world a better place through the power of co-creation.

Introduction

In today's fast-paced world, life can get the better of you, and you end up feeling stressed out, overwhelmed and exhausted mentally, emotionally and physically. You might be among those suffering from 'the overwhelmed syndrome:' you have too many obligations or responsibilities and there is not enough time in the day. As a result, you have lost all sense of control over your life, emotions, energy levels, resilience and inner peace.

I personally remember a time in my life when I was going through the same sense of 'overwhelm.' I was questioning the purpose of my own existence and the meaning of life on earth.

"God, there's got to be more. This cannot be it for my life."
– Howard Thurman

Like Howard Thurman, this was my plea in my mid-thirties. I was going through a period of existential angst and I found myself in a dark hole mentally and emotionally. My sense of 'not belonging,' 'feeling lost,' and 'lacking clarity' meant that I felt disconnected from the world around me.

I was unhappy, despite the fact that I had a wonderful family, a comfortable life and very nice friends. I believed deep in my heart that there was more to life than what my life was back then. It felt as if my present-day existence had no meaning and therefore that living was pointless. The fact is I was not fulfilled.

These crippling thoughts lasted for about three months. I was yearning for a more fulfilling life. Even though I felt out of place on planet Earth, I had hope and I had faith.

I knew that the only solution for my lack of fulfilment and contentment was a spiritual one and that it was time for me to look within.

I raised the same questions that the 19th century philosopher and father of Existentialism, Soren Kierkegaard, asked himself in his letter to his friend Peter Wilhelm Lund dated 31 August 1835:

> "What I really lack is to be clear in my mind what I am to do, not what I am to know, except in so far as a certain knowledge must precede every action. The thing is to understand myself, to see what God really wishes me to do: the thing is to find a truth which is true for me, to find the idea for which I can live and die. I certainly do not deny that I still recognize an imperative of knowledge and that through it one can work upon men, but it must be taken up into my life, and that is what I now recognize as the most important thing."

Like Soren Kierkegaard, my desire to self-realize and to give meaning to my life, in order to justify my existence, was profound. I turned to God for guidance one night and my prayer for clarity was answered. I asked: "Beloved God please reveal to me, in my dreams, what my divine life purpose is." I remember waking up in the middle of the night as I received this guidance loud and clear: "Your life purpose is to enhance people's lives."

This was for me a great night of revelation. Finally, I could see the light because I now had a direction and an understanding of my higher purpose. I believe that this particular time of my life marked the beginning of my spiritual journey and fulfilment.

I came to realize and believe that my life would have more meaning if I made a difference in other people's lives. Even though I did not know how I was going to enhance people's lives I simply trusted the guidance I was given. Today, nothing gives me more joy than living a purposeful life.

Yes! To Love™ is the result of my work as a Reiki healer, transformational and success life coach. I believe it is my mission to help as many people as possible find inner peace and live a happy, fulfilling and meaningful life.

The purpose of this book is to help you grow in awareness so that you can live the magical, balanced and harmonious life that you deserve. Throughout the following pages, it is my intention that you get inspired and motivated to transform your life for greater everyday life balance.

Yes! To Love™ is divided into 10 chapters:

- ♥ In Chapter 1: you are invited and encouraged to live a more balanced life.
- ♥ In Chapter 2: you are guided to come out of your comfort zone.
- ♥ In Chapter 3: you learn the secrets to self-transformation.
- ♥ In Chapter 4: you learn the easiest path to personal transformation.
- ♥ In Chapter 5: you learn the secrets to success.
- ♥ In Chapter 6: you learn practical ways to live in the now.

- ♥ In Chapter 7: you learn practical ways to improve your mind power.
- ♥ In Chapter 8: you learn practical ways to uplift your body.
- ♥ In Chapter 9: you learn practical ways to uplift your spirit.
- ♥ In Chapter 10: you learn about the power of love.

This book will help you improve the quality of your life by giving you access to practical ways and tools you can use to enjoy everyday life balance.

With Love and Gratitude

Pascale D. Gibon

PART ONE

CHAPTER 1

Living a Balanced Life Every Day

1. On the road to greater life balance

According to HeartMath Institute: "Millions of people today have reached the point at which everything has become too much." In today's society people are stressed and overwhelmed due to the pressure of everyday life. There are demands at home, school, work and socially. You are reading *Yes! To Love™ - The Ultimate Guide to Personal Transformation for Everyday Life Balance* because you want to reach a greater state of emotional, mental and physical balance in order not to cope with life but to fully embrace the gift of life. This is your time, not to survive but to finally live happily. It is your intention from now on to find balance every day.

Yes! To Love™ has been written on the premise that:

- ♥ You are in a state of wholeness and completeness when you find inner peace and when you are balanced.
- ♥ You find inner peace and you are balanced when you say *Yes! to love.*

This *Ultimate Guide to Personal Transformation for Everyday Life Balance* takes you from a place of imbalance in your life to a place where you feel more resilient and better mentally, emotionally and physically more often. Therefore, the transformational decision you have to make is to commit to living your life from a place of greater love from now on. Throughout the next pages you will learn how you can achieve this step by step.

Yes! To Love™ - The Ultimate Guide to Personal Transformation for Everyday Life Balance has been written for people who:

- ♥ want more happiness in their life
- ♥ have a highly stressful life and want to do something about it
- ♥ want to be in a state of bliss and inner peace most of the time
- ♥ want to regain control over their life
- ♥ are willing to learn how to best respond to difficult situations
- ♥ want to fall back in love with their life

You will discover simple shifts and adjustments, which you are encouraged to introduce in your life. These might be for you new or forgotten habits. As it takes time to introduce new habits, I recommend that you do so step by step.

> *Henrietta chose to transform her life in order to experience wholeness, completeness and love. Her childhood memories were painful due to a dysfunctional household. Her parents were both very unhappy and argued most of the time. This really affected Henrietta's love relationships and her relationship with her parents. It was causing her emotional distress until the day she decided to do something about it. She chose to look at her situation with the eyes of love by making the decision to*

understand her parents better and to forgive them. After several months of self-reflection, healing and coaching she had a significant breakthrough; she improved her relationship with her parents and felt much more at peace. Henrietta made the decision to improve her life. She was willing and able to do so.

"If you change the way you look at things,
the things you look at change."
– Dr. Wayne Dyer

2. Find peace within

Jonathan is one of five children and he had a rather conflicting relationship with one of his siblings, which affected the family dynamic. I could hear Jonathan's anger each time he talked about his sibling. I suggested he changed the way he perceived his brother altogether by sending him love and forgiving him for whatever he had or not done. As a result of him sending love to his brother and healing their relationship the latter stopped being negative toward him and became more understanding. Jonathan found greater peace within.

In order to achieve everyday life balance, you have to be in a certain way. Indeed, it is an internal process which manifests itself externally. When you find peace within you find peace without.

It is Albert Einstein who said that: "Insanity is doing the same thing over and over again and expecting different results."

To live an everyday balanced life you must grow in self-awareness and remain in a state of peace at all times. How do you do this?

- ♥ Do you get angry easily?
- ♥ Do you get frustrated easily?
- ♥ Are you impatient?
- ♥ Do you get a sense of 'overwhelm' easily?

Such feelings and emotions create a restless mind and interfere with your inner peace.

Whenever you are faced with anger, frustration find peace by saying Yes! to love. You can ask yourself this simple question: "What would love do?"

Whenever you become impatient find peace by saying: "Am I embracing the present moment fully?"

Where there is disharmony peace is to enter.

Your inner peace will resonate inside and out. In other words, when you remain peaceful your environment will be affected by your state of calmness. One of my mentors, Bob Proctor, says: "We don't need to slow down we need to calm down."

The feeling of contentment and inner peace derives from the belief and faith that there is always a spiritual solution to any problem you might face.

When you adopt inner peace, in every aspect of your life, this becomes your foundation for a balanced life.

"Be at peace with yourself and choose in favour of peace at all times."
– Pascale D. Gibon

3. Your new way of overcoming obstacles

Tom was caught up in a never-ending spiral of disastrous love relationships. He went from failure to failure and he recognized that he found himself in a vicious circle; all his love relationships followed the same pattern and ended miserably. Tom realized that nothing would change until he changed and broke this negative pattern. He decided to learn from his mistakes this time around and to improve himself in order to improve his love life. With some coaching help from me, he now has the courage to dig deep as he is on the path of self-healing and self-reflection for a more balanced life.

We commonly feel defeated when we face difficult situations that cause us stress. By obstacles I mean the things that stand in the way of your inner peace and well-being. Generally, this is due to low self-esteem, fear, and the belief that nothing can go right. In this case it is important that you change your way of thinking.

You attract what you think about therefore by allowing yourself to succeed and to let go of fear you create a new and desired reality for yourself. Failure is always an opportunity to do better next time, to seek a better solution, to strive further, to become a better person, a better parent, a better partner, brother or sister etc. Your wisdom will have to come into play and how you choose to respond to the problem at hand will determine whether you are able to handle it or not.

It is easy to dwell on problems however it is even easier to take steps to find remarkable solutions. Indeed, when we dwell on problems we are not actually seeking solutions and, consequently, the problems tend to escalate in accordance with the way we perceive them. This was Tom's challenge until he realized what was happening and he decided to take steps. Remember that there is a spiritual solution to every obstacle or problem you may face therefore asking yourself the right questions will make all the difference.

For example, instead of: "There is a problem here; I do not know what to do" Ask yourself the following questions: "How could I solve this present problem?" "What is there for me to learn in this particular situation?" With this attitude of openness, you are seeking solutions by asking the right question. Tom knew that there were lessons for him to learn because the same problems seemed to repeat themselves from one relationship to the next.

Obstacles are always new lessons to be learned and opportunity for growth. You find balance when you view these obstacles from a place of acceptance and you seek solutions. Generally, the more we complain the more the obstacles remain because our attitude is one of resistance. On the other hand, the more we accept what is the more we find inner peace and solutions abound. It is like a brainstorming when things you never thought of suddenly become relevant to your particular problem or obstacle.

"If you want small changes in your life, work on your attitude. But if you want big and primary changes, work on your paradigm."
– Stephen Covey

4. Healing your inner child

We all have a story that shapes our life experience, our beliefs, our personality, our memory and our uniqueness. You certainly have your own story. I mentioned at the beginning of this book that everyday life balance is an inside job which then resonates out. Therefore, it is important that you comfort, nurture and heal your inner child particularly in times when you feel imbalanced in your life.

Your inner child is the real you. It is the child who needs more attention, more praise, more recognition, more acknowledgment and more love. As you nurture your inner child you can reconnect with the things you love or the things you love doing, which you might have neglected or stopped doing.

For example, it could be something creative or as simple as a stroll in the park. It could be cooking a wonderful meal or travelling somewhere new. A friend of mine makes it a priority to travel somewhere new every month and this is her way of healing her inner child and finding inner balance.

It seems important to accept that we all have a story of suffering one way or another. However, from a spiritual viewpoint without your story there will be no need for you to grow and to heal your inner child. Nurturing and remembering your inner child are your ways of connecting with your truth. The essence of your being lies in the inner child. Connecting with and nurturing that child is what makes the difference between happiness and unhappiness. Remembering who you are, what you love, what you are good at and your values are your ways of caring for your inner child.

During a Reiki workshop, I remember the exercise our Reiki master did with one of the participants. This particular participant was a perfectionist. According to my Reiki Master, perfectionists tend to look for imperfections. In order for him to let go of perfectionism she asked him to attend the workshop the next day wearing different coloured socks. He actually did and felt much better for it. He was carefree, he felt comfortable with it. He did not mind if he was being judged or not. He had the courage to take his inner child to play.

It is time for you to reconnect with your inner child and to take him or her to play.

Exercise 1

What could you do today to nurture your inner child by taking him or her to play?

The author Debbie Ford put a great emphasis on keeping her inner child happy. Every day she did something for herself that brought her joy.

"In my soul, I am still that small child who did not care about anything else but the beautiful colors of a rainbow."
– Papiha Ghosh

5. Understanding the three-step process for everyday life balance

My friend Chinmai Swamy, who is an author and mountaineer, always says: "First thing first, choose your mountain" or choose where you want to be. How high you climb your chosen mountain will depend entirely on your attitude which is a combination of your thoughts, feelings and actions.

Like Vera Nazarian put it: "If you are faced with a mountain, you have several options. You can climb it and cross to the other side. You can go around it. You can dig under it. You can fly over it. You can blow it up. You can ignore it and pretend it's not there. You can turn around and go back the way you came.

Or you can stay on the mountain and make it your home."

- ♥ Choose your mountain.
- ♥ Take actions to reach the top.
- ♥ Make it your home and enjoy the view.

In order to make it your home and to reach the top you will have to make some changes and sacrifices. Those sacrifices relate to your willingness to give up something of a lower nature in order to obtain something of a higher nature. Furthermore, you will have to release the chains that hold you back. The ultimate price is freedom.

By reading this book you have chosen your mountain for a miraculous, enjoyable and balanced life as well as the achievement of your dreams. You are whole and perfect therefore the three-step process for everyday life balance includes the mind body and spirit.

As you grow in self-awareness for a more balanced life, it is important that you engage all three. In order to reach the top of your chosen mountain you will have to be conditioned, prepared and fit.

- ♥ Your spirit is conditioned to Barry Finlay's idea that: "Every mountain top is within reach if you just keep climbing."

Once you start climbing the mountain it is easy to give up and harder to keep going. However, you must know that the universe will support you on your journey for no mountain is high enough.

- ♥ Your mental activity will falter or motivate you.

Therefore, your results will be dependent upon you either thinking "I don't know if I will have the stamina to reach the top" or "Come what may I will succeed and nothing can stop me." Keeping your goal in mind and visualizing that you have reached the top victorious, with a big smile on your face and a sense of accomplishment will support you on your journey.

- ♥ Your physical level of fitness and conditioning will determine how far you will climb to reap the benefits of the ultimate price; the most spectacular view and your desired results.

In the light of everyday life balance, you climb the mountain step by step and it is important that you keep this image in mind as you embark on your new path.

"It is not the mountain we conquer but ourselves."
– Edmund Hillary

6. It is time to say Yes! to love

Benjamin had a conflicting relationship with his son. He was under the impression that his son was resentful somehow regarding a past event. His son's mood was changeable. One day he would be kind to his father and the next his mood would be the opposite. I suggested to Benjamin to change his attitude in order to change the energy around their relationship. All he had to do was to be more loving by sending more love to his son through prayer, visualization, and meditation or simply face to face when they met. He chose to act differently toward his son and to clearly show him that he loves him. The last time I spoke to Benjamin he was amazed by how the dynamic of their relationship changed and he now truly enjoys a harmonious and loving relationship with his son.

In order to experience a more miraculous life as well as more bliss, balance and peace in your life, this book is an invitation to you to include more love in your life by saying Yes! to love. Mahatma Gandhi said: "Where there is love there is life."

Indeed, everyday life balance is achieved with love insight daily. Should your life be imbalanced right now you are invited to live your life with greater love for yourself, for others, for the things you do, for the environment and for the entire planet.

As you live from this perspective of love daily, it is important that you self-reflect and ask yourself:

- How much love have I given today?
- Have I responded to a particular situation from a place of love?
- Have I shown kindness and compassion to others?
- Was I a beacon of love?
- Was I loving and loveable?
- Have I been kind to myself?
- Have I expressed appreciation?

It is only when you embrace love fully and when you deepen your 'well of love' daily that you find greater harmony in your life. Should you feel that you have not said Yes! to love today, it is time to clear your heart of any debris or obstructions to love. Practical ways in which you can do so will be revealed in Chapter 10, entitled: The Power of Love.

When you say Yes! to love you embrace life fully and you let go of fear. You trust that everything in your life is in perfect divine order. Say Yes! to love in order to fall back in love with your life.

"Where there is love there is life."
– Mahatma Gandhi

Bonus #1
Discover The 7 Success Habits For Inner Peace, Joy & Happiness

Get your pdf copy free at:

http://www.yestolovebook.com

CHAPTER 2

Coming out of Your Comfort Zone

1. How to overcome everyday challenges

The Oxford Dictionary gives the following definition of a challenge: "A call to someone to participate in a competitive situation or fight to decide who is superior in terms of ability or strength."

It is time to wake up to a new awareness: according to Universal Wisdom you are never given a challenge in life that you cannot solve. You are always given two choices: to let it drift with the hope that it will go away or to act by taking the necessary measure to tackle it. It is your strength and courage, which are being tested each time.

When you seek greater life balance you are competing with two forces: your critical voice and your wise voice. The former will try to protect you by creating fear with affirmations such as: "Who do you think you are to come out of your comfort zone?! Everything is fine as it is." The latter will help you to see the top of the mountain and thus increase your belief in greater life balance. You can choose to acknowledge your critical voice but to follow your wise voice.

The extent of your challenge will be dependent upon your need for growth in order to achieve greater life balance. Indeed, your own growth blueprint determines what you need to improve. In Tom's case there was an imbalance in his life between his ideal relationship and the ones he was habitually attracting.

Your personal growth will be determined by your aspirations, intentions and actions.

In most cases challenges in life are a direct response to our deepest fear. The fear of failure, of success, of saying the wrong thing, of not being good enough, beautiful enough, smart or young enough etc. As a consequence, your particular fear will manifest in everything you do. It will challenge you until one day you wake up and realize that this is the problem you need to solve in this lifetime as it is a direct expression and manifestation of what Master Ruyho Okawa calls "your soul's tendency." For example, if your fear is that you are not good enough, you will meet people who will undermine you or praise you. The purpose of the people who will undermine you is to teach you how to be assertive, to express your greatness and to share your personal gifts. On the other hand, the purpose of the people who will praise you is to recognize within yourself that you are good enough by accepting their praise as true. In both cases you have met your teachers. Once you have tackled this challenge a new challenge will present itself and assist you in your growth.

How you respond to everyday challenges will determine your results of balance or imbalance. When you come out of your comfort zone you become more in alignment with a balanced life because you allow yourself to grow.

"Life is a song - sing it. Life is a game - play it. Life is a challenge - meet it. Life is a dream - realize it. Life is a sacrifice - offer it. Life is love - enjoy it."
– Sai Baba

2. You can do it!

By reading this book you made the resolve to create more balance in your life. I appeal to you as a creative being who creates their life on a day to day basis. You harness your creative power when you grow in awareness. Therefore, what do you become aware of when you want to have more balance in your life? You become aware of your inner power, of the power of thoughts. Your inner strength is what guides you on a day to day basis. There is no reward for playing it small and for continuing to live an imbalanced life.

You have now become aware that you can change your reality as you wish, for you are the creator of your reality. I know beyond the shadow of a doubt that as you put your intention and attention on more balance in your life from the inside out, changes for the better will occur in your life unexpectedly, in various shapes and forms. You can decide now to set the intention to create your balanced life by design and to experience it the way you want to live it.

It is encouraging to know that there is always hope. It is true that we are creatures of habits and it is those habits that no longer serve you that create the imbalance.

Wayne Dyer explained it as follows: "The single most important tool to being in balance is knowing that you and only you are responsible for the imbalance between what you dream your life is meant to be, and the daily habits that drain life from that dream."

Alice is self-employed and she has the tendency to be fashionably late for all of her appointments. This created an imbalance in her life because her lateness stressed her out.

If, like Alice, you have the habit of being late for your appointment you can change this habit by getting up earlier, by leaving home earlier and by arriving on time for all of your appointments. You can make the conscious effort right now to change your habit of lateness by implementing the recommendations above.

♥ What new habit have you chosen to adopt?

Are you ready? – The answer is YES.

"One of the things that make us so special is our ability to adapt, to transform, to manipulate objects or ideas to produce something more pleasing or useful."
– Tony Robbins

3. Welcoming the new you

It is worth mentioning again that human beings are creatures of habits. Welcoming the new you offers a new vision for your life as your intention is to have more balance in your life.

By welcoming the new you simply welcome a better, happier and more truthful version of you.

The new you is not someone who lives in frustration because you are not getting things done, things are not working out your way and/or you are overwhelmed. The new you is someone who accepts to harness their power of creation for greater life balance.

The new you is someone who chooses to take action in order to make significant changes in your life. What actions have we covered so far:

- Say Yes! to love from now on.
- Embrace the gift of life fully.
- Cultivate a more positive attitude to life.
- Contemplate inner peace.
- Make transformational decisions.
- Change your perception.
- Take your inner child out to play.
- Change the daily habits that no longer serve you and create imbalances.
- Harness your inner power of creation.

Olympic athletes who train for hours on end always have a burning desire to win. The British Olympic champion Mo Farah is exemplary. He was determined to return to Britain with a gold medal. In 2011, he competed for the 10,000m at Daegu World Championship in Athletics. It was painful to watch yet so exhilarating! His 200m sprint finish to race away from his competitors meant that the gold medal was his. However, as he closed on the finish line with 50m remaining he got beaten by the Ethiopian Ibrahim Jeilan. This is the race Mo Farah wanted to focus on, he said after the race: "It's a great feeling once you cross that line in first place – an unbelievable feeling. I didn't have that feeling today." In spite of his near victory, Mo Farah knew he could win a gold medal and that he should not miss this chance. Through sheer determination, he decided to run the 5,000m a week later. He not only took gold in the Men's 5,000m final but also became the 5th male athlete to complete the long-distance double at the championships. He returned to England with the gold medal and fulfilled his dream.

"For last year's words belong to last year's language. And next year's words await another voice. And to make an end is to make a beginning."
– T. S Eliot

4. Reclaiming your inner power

When you watch a performance by Cirque du Soleil you gain a better understanding of the extent of human power and potential. You are amazed by the strength of the human mind, body and spirit. You even wonder how it is possible that human beings can achieve such physical prowess. It is first created in the mind.

As you explore the world within, you must recognize and harness your inner power. You hear two voices: that of the EGO (Edging God Out according to Wayne Dyer), which will challenge you and tell you why you 'can't,' "You are not ready for change," "This will not work" etc. and your real voice stemming from your inner power, which will encourage you, motivate you, inspire you, take you a step further and higher, assist you and nurture you in many ways. You reclaim your inner power when you choose to follow your real voice. Your inner power is the truth of your being. There lies only joy and contentment and a field of limitless possibilities.

When you reclaim your inner power you do not let your emotions control you, you control them. You are disempowered and you become a victim when you dwell on your sorrows and pain because you have created attachments to these emotions. You are powerful beyond measure, just hold this thought for a moment and like Napoleon Hill said become aware that: "Whatever the mind can conceive and believe, it can achieve."

Exercise 2

Remember a time when you felt on top of the world. It was a very happy time. Visualize this moment, see what you see, feel what you feel, hear what you hear and let this emotion of happiness and well-being envelop your entire body.

As you create greater balance in your life you learn to listen to the real voice more and more, to correct any negative thinking that is not serving you and to live in a field of endless possibilities. When you reclaim your inner power you become consciously aware that there is no limit to what you can create. This state of mind will help you transition from a place of pain to a place of power and from a place of fear to a place of true happiness, inner peace and contentment.

"Your ego cries with 'look out!' because is it afraid and because it believes 'everything good is outside.' Your spirit sings 'Look within!' because it knows you are complete and whole and happy already."
– Robert Holden in "Happiness Now!"

5. Are you being you?

I recall reading Simon's story in Caroline Myss' book "Why People Don't Heal and How They Can." Simon was a lawyer because his father was a judge. Simon was told from a very early age by his father that his dream was to work in a father-and-son law practice. Simon became a lawyer at 26, got married at 27 and became a father at 29. "By the time Simon was 34 he was on the verge of a nervous breakdown. He could no longer relate to his wife, either verbally or sexually, and he could no longer handle the responsibilities of his job."

Simon did not realize until he was into his early thirties that he might be allowed to have ambitions of his own for he had never been given freedom of choice in any area of his life. He started therapy work and during the next week, he found it almost impossible to sleep at night. "His thoughts returned to his childhood, and to all the plans and expectations that had been predetermined for him. He began to experience rage such as he had never known before. Afraid of what he might say to his father – or of holding in what he would like to say – Simon avoided communication with him altogether." As he was taken into the journey of self-discovery, Simon was finally able to tap into his authentic self and to know his real self.

Are you being you or are you living someone else's dreams? In other words, is your life a reflection of your heart's desires? It is difficult to live authentically and in balance when you are living someone else's dreams.

I recommend that you strive to follow your dreams because this is when you are the happiest and on purpose.

What is your entitlement as someone who seeks greater balance in your life?

- ♥ You are free to recognize and reclaim your power of creation.
- ♥ You are free to choose greater inner peace and harmony in your life.
- ♥ You are free to radiate love from the depth of your being and out.

However, you might sense from the depth of your heart that your life right now is not in alignment with your dreams.

"To help yourself, you must be yourself. Be the best that you can be. When you make a mistake, learn from it, pick yourself up and move on."
– Dave Pelzer

6. Honouring your Self

Rachel always said that she wanted to get married again, despite a divorce a few years back. One day she made the decision to put a lot of energy into her love life after 'kissing many frogs.' She sat down and thought clearly, truthfully and in detail about what type of relationship she was willing to commit to this time. Six months later she met her husband, who she now calls her soul mate, and they are happily married.

When life circumstances and events put you off balance and create disharmony, you can reconnect to the higher part of you in order to find inner peace and contentment. For example, you could sit down somewhere quiet, close your eyes and take a few deep breaths in order to reconnect to your higher self. Each time that you are being challenged, return to spirit. Ask yourself: "How am I feeling?" If you are not feeling well, recognize what thought or belief has engendered your discomfort.

You are a Bright Shining Star and this is my invitation to you to honour your inner diamond and to let it shine. In order to honour your truth of joy, peace, and harmony you choose to let go and release anything that is not in alignment with these qualities.

In order to honour your true self, you are willing to let your true nature shine brightly. Each time you reconnect to your true nature you experience God and you become one with God. Allow yourself to feel the love in your heart.

One of my mentors, Bob Proctor, says it best: "Most people are extras in their own movie." It is time now to play the leading role in your own movie.

"When you connect to your inner truth you reconnect in fact to a place of love, harmony, and peace."
– Pascale D. Gibon

Bonus #2
Assertiveness Now! Breakthrough Session

Reserve your 30-minute Assertiveness Now! Breakthrough Session (limited spaces) at:

http://www.yestolovebook.com

CHAPTER 3

Secrets to Self-Transformation

1. Clarify your personal values

In order to reach your goals, it is important to know where you are right now. We all have personal values, which drive our behaviour. Your personal values clearly indicate what is most important to you in your life.

- ♥ What are your personal values?
- ♥ What are your priorities?
- ♥ What is most important to you?

Knowing your values will also help you determine the kind of person you are, what makes you tick, what is and not acceptable to you.

You can do the following exercise to assess where you are with regard to your personal values:

Exercise 3

Make a list of your top 10 most important values. Put the top 5 in priority order and assess whether they are present in your life right now. If not, how could you introduce them in your life?

There might be an imbalance in your life because you are not in alignment with your personal values. When you find yourself in this situation it can be disheartening and hard work to sustain.

For example, within a work environment, you might be surrounded by people with totally different values or you might realize that you no longer share the ethos of the company you work for. It might be difficult for you to evolve in such an inadequate environment. Such a situation can be draining and stressful because you try hard to fit in.

Generally, you are more comfortable with people you share the same values with. If it is your current situation great, if not I suggest you evaluate whether the imbalance comes from the fact that you do not share the same values.

When you know your own values you know what works and what does not work for you in your life. When you are totally aligned with you core personal values you live a happier, less stressful and more balanced and authentic life. I suggest that you rise to the challenge by making the conscious effort to do exercise 3 as a starting point.

"If it doesn't challenge you it does not change you."
– Socrates

Secret #1 to Self-Transformation: Know your personal values

2. Make the decision to change now

Perhaps you are reading this book because you have told yourself finally that enough is enough and it is time for you to get more balance in your life.

You feel that:

- ♥ things are not working out the way you want them to
- ♥ there is too much imbalance in your life
- ♥ no matter how hard you try you do not seem to get anywhere
- ♥ you are lost and you do not know what to do next
- ♥ you cannot see clearly the solutions to your problems
- ♥ you are going round and round in circles and you do not seem to have a breakthrough
- ♥ you feel very stressed out and it is getting the better of you
- ♥ help is needed

You are tired of this lack of inner peace and this has got to change once and for all. You know in your heart of hearts that you deserve a better life and a better life awaits you.

For transformation to occur you not only tell yourself that 'enough is enough' but you also decide to change what needs to be changed once and for all.

"The person who fails to develop their ability to make decisions is doomed because indecision sets up internal conflicts which can, without warning, escalate into all out mental and emotional wars. Psychiatrists have a name to describe these internal wars, it is ambivalence. My Oxford Dictionary tells me that ambivalence is the coexistence in one person of opposite feelings toward the same objective."
– Bob Proctor

Secret #2 to Self-Transformation: Make the decision to change now

3. Follow the road of least resistance

As Albert Einstein put it: "No problem can be solved from the same level of consciousness that created it." Indeed as you make the decision to transform your life, you have decided, as well, to think and act differently and to become a new person.

Since you are now embarking on this new transformational journey, I extend the invitation to you to decide right now to consciously:

♥ Let go of beating yourself up.

♥ Allow yourself to acknowledge and to let go of any frustration, worry, fear or anxiety you may feel right now.

♥ Let go of any disharmony, imbalance, incongruence in your life.

♥ Refrain from expressing any criticism, judgement, dissatisfaction toward yourself and others.

In this light, I invite you to embark on a new journey of transformation where you will discover a way of being which brings you inner peace and is in total harmony with your true nature; your divine nature.

You know that you are ready for change, however you are still pondering: "Can I sincerely find inner peace?", "What am I to do next?" Inner peace is within you and it is your oneness with God. All that is necessary is for you to awaken to your

God-given gifts. The following chapters will show you how.

***"Discover your truth and be its full expression.
God's wish for you is to be happy."
- Pascale D. Gibon***

Secret #3 to Self-Transformation: Follow the road of least resistance

4. Look within

Your outer world is a reflection of your inner world; therefore, whenever you contemplate change it is important first to look within. This is probably one of the most challenging things to do because it requires you to be honest with yourself. You must understand that whatever you uncover within it is there to help you move forward in your life and to bring change.

By reading this book you have chosen to:

♥ live your life authentically

♥ surrender to your higher self

♥ let go of any control your ego may hold over you

Specifically, you have chosen to live your life from a higher perspective of understanding; from a spiritual viewpoint. Moreover, you have chosen to be free as you follow your truth; your heart.

Like Wayne Dyer put it: "Don't die with that music still in you;" the life you truly wanted to live, the things you wanted to do and the dreams you did not fulfil. What is most important is that you awaken to the truth that you have not lived your life authentically until now and this may be the cause of your suffering and unhappiness.

You live authentically when:

- ♥ your intentions are pure
- ♥ you are honest with yourself
- ♥ you live a fulfilling life
- ♥ you follow your truth
- ♥ you follow your heart's desires and let go of fear
- ♥ you show compassion toward others
- ♥ the only thing you wish to give is love
- ♥ you choose to forgive
- ♥ you choose to serve
- ♥ you live your purpose
- ♥ you follow your intuitive inner voice
- ♥ you surrender your entire being to the Divine
- ♥ you allow the real you to shine
- ♥ you let go of your EGO (Edging God Out) and let your higher self lead the way
- ♥ you are able to tell yourself at the end of your life that you have truly lived

"Do what you know you have to do to feel whole, to feel complete, and to feel as if you're fulfilling your destiny. You'll never be at peace if you don't get that music out and let it play. Don't die with that music still in you."
– Wayne Dyer

Secret #4 to Self-Transformation: Look within

5. Let go of limiting habits

Firstly, what you have learnt so far is that for transformation to occur you must make the committed decision to change, to identify what needs to be changed and to take the necessary actions to implement the changes.

Secondly, your committed decision to change is also accompanied by the commitment to let go of:

- ♥ anything that does not work in your life
- ♥ any obstacles that undermine your inner peace
- ♥ any imbalance that creates too much frustration, stress and discomfort
- ♥ a way of being and doing which are not congruent with your desire for greater balance in your life

For transformation to occur you must let go of any attachment to the past and choose the immediate moment for a better future. However, when unpleasant memories of the past creep back in, you are now consciously aware that you are hanging on to them and you choose to let them go.

Thirdly, you must identify and let go of any habits that no longer serve you as they create too much imbalance in your life.

Exercise 4

What habits are you to let go of?

As an example, the runner Mo Farah chose to run the 5,000m the day after his near success, at 10,000m, at Daegu World Championship in Athletics in 2011. He chose not to be deterred by anything that would be in the way of his success like discouragement, lack of stamina, depleted hunger for success or decreased desire. As a result, he won the gold medal.

His state of mind could have been:

"I am shattered," "I was so close!" "I cannot do this,"

"I no longer have the strength or the energy," "I have failed."

Instead his attitude was a positive one:

"Bring it on!" "I am a winner," "I can do this," "Nothing is stopping me now," "Nothing will get in my way."

His mental and emotional strength resulted in his strong desire to win.

"The truth is, unless you let go, unless you forgive yourself, unless you forgive the situation, unless you realize that the situation is over, you cannot move forward."
– Steve Maraboli

Secret #5 to Self-Transformation: Let go of limiting habits

6. Let your inner diamond shine

In the same way a caterpillar transforms itself into a butterfly you can visualize your own personal transformation whereby you allow your inner diamond to shine.

Let us use the life cycle of the butterfly as an analogy between the workings of nature and your own transformation:

The first stage: the egg. The tiny caterpillar to be is growing inside of it.

The second stage: the larva (caterpillar). At this stage, the caterpillar is mainly eating so that it can grow quickly. The caterpillar grows by shedding its outgrown skin.

The third stage: the pupa (chrysalis). Inside the pupa the caterpillar is rapidly changing. The old body of the caterpillar undergoes metamorphosis to emerge as a beautiful butterfly. As the caterpillar releases itself from its silky cocoon it finds freedom and blossoms into a beautiful butterfly.

The fourth stage: the adult butterfly. The butterfly has come out of the chrysalis and it takes three to four hours to learn how to fly.

Since there is so much we can learn from nature here is your own butterfly-like metamorphosis.

The first stage: you are at the starting point; you have identified that it is time to create greater balance in your life.

The second stage: you are feeding yourself with the necessary knowledge to find greater balance in your life. Like the caterpillar you grow by solving your workbook of life step by step.

The third stage: as you grow in awareness you are rapidly changing.

The fourth stage: you are now free to fly and to let your inner diamond shine brightly.

Since you are reading this book, similar to the butterfly you are going through the transformation process. When you choose inner peace and more balance in your life you will also find freedom from fear, worry and stress. When you are free you shine like a diamond inside and out.

***"Personal transformation can and does have global effects.
As we go, so goes the world, for the world is us.
The revolution that will save the world
is ultimately a personal one."
– Marianne Williamson***

Secret #6 to Self-Transformation: Let your inner diamond shine

CHAPTER 4

Secrets to Your Success

1. Learn to say 'no'

You might feel that there is not enough time in the day if there are a lot of pressure and demands on your time in your personal and professional life. If you are a 'people pleaser' remember to set boundaries by learning to say 'no.'

There is no need to say 'yes' if your decision will increase your stress levels and thus your health, imbalance and well-being. I remember reading Rosie's story in a British newspaper regarding work pressure in the City of London and the high levels of people suffering from depression.

> *Rosie was an analyst in the City until she got completely burnt out. She was put under tremendous pressure to perform. She was young and she had to prove herself. The 26-year-old was working 12 to 14 hours a day and her evenings were spent at internal networking events or wooing potential clients over dinner. She managed this work pattern with only six hours of sleep a night until it caught up with her. She no longer had a personal life, her relationship with her boyfriend collapsed, she was struggling to sleep and she was constantly anxious. She fell into depression and could no longer cope with life. She also became very tearful, unhappy, overwhelmed and out of control over her life. She was relieved when she was made redundant from her job because she was no longer functioning as a human being and able to get out of*

bed in the morning. She has now rebuilt her life after some counselling and a 6-month break. Rosie retrained in nutrition and has now set up her own company.

Rosie took advantage of her new work situation to change her life around. You are responsible for your own life and you have the freedom to choose the life you desire completely: an unhappy life or a fulfilling one. Even though the job was paying well and was high profile Rosie was unhappy with the demands of the job. She could no longer differentiate between her profession and personal life. It happens that the decision to change career was made for her.

When you know that something would take up too much of your time it is completely alright to say 'no' if you give a reason why. Let us take the example of a work environment situation. You are completely overwhelmed with heavy workload yet your Director comes to you with additional work. It is perfectly ok to communicate effectively by asking what is the priority and what should you focus on.

I remember 'listening' to a conversation a young lady had at the post office. She was talking to someone on the phone about her day at work. She said that her boss tends to come to the office late and therefore that she has to work overtime despite the fact that she had been in since the morning. She said her boss called her up to ask her to stay behind because he had to finish his project today and he would come at 4pm. This young lady was getting married and had an appointment at 6pm related to the wedding. She told her boss that she would not be able to work late and whether he could come earlier so that she could leave on time. His answer was 'but I have a deadline today!'

The decision to live a balanced life in your terms is entirely yours. This requires some adjustments in your way of thinking, being and doing.

"Letting go helps us to live in a more peaceful state of mind and helps restore our balance. It allows others to be responsible for themselves and for us to take our hands off situations that do not belong to us. This frees us from unnecessary stress."
– Melodie Beattie

Secret #1 to success in Everyday Life Balance™: Learn to say 'no'

2. The law of cause and effect

The law of cause and effect dictates that you are at cause when you take full responsibility for whatever happens in your life and you are at effect when you blame others. Since you are the architect of your own life, you must take 100% responsibility for whatever happens.

When you take full responsibility for your life you feel empowered, you feel free and you are in acceptance of what is. We often blame others for what happens to us until we realize that, maybe, we attracted the situation in the first place, through our thoughts or our actions. According to the spiritual leader Ryuho Okawa: "Our life is a workbook of problems that need to be solved." In this light, you must accept that whatever happens in your life is intended as part of your personal growth.

Responsibility is your ability to respond. How you respond to your life's events will determine the type of life you experience. Your commitment is to take full responsibility for your life, without blaming your circumstances such as: your parents, your colleagues, your partner etc. You will learn throughout this book that by adopting The Everyday Life Balance Process you will grow in awareness and increase your ability to respond.

For example, two people faced with the same problem, like a train running late, will act differently according to their level of awareness.

One person will react by becoming agitated, frustrated, impatient and even angry. The other one will respond by remaining calm and thinking that there is nothing they can do about it and therefore they choose to read a book, for example, while they are waiting patiently. The latter is more in alignment with The Everyday Life Balance Process. How they respond to the event will affect the way they spend the rest of the day.

Exercise 5

Take a moment to think about how you would have reacted or responded to the situation. Please note that if your reaction would have been similar to that of the first passenger this would have increased your stress levels.

"The price of greatness is responsibility."
– Winston Churchill

Secret #2 to success in Everyday Life Balance™: Take 100% responsibility for your life

3. Be willing to fall forward

When you wish to obtain everyday balance, falling forward is acceptable. You can ask very successful people in any field and they will tell you that they failed miserably several times before they became successful.

The Wright Brothers, who conceived the first aircraft that could be controlled while in the air, failed countless times. In fact, their idea of creating the first controlled flying machine in 1899 took six years to become a fact in 1905.

Failure is good because it is actually a way of getting feedback and moving forward. For example, if you want to bring balance in your physical well-being by reaching your perfect weight and you have failed miserably, this setback could indicate the following:

- you have not reached your goal therefore something needs to be changed
- little adjustments might make a difference
- you spent more days eating an imbalanced diet than a balanced one therefore you could change your eating habits
- you might need to examine your will power and daily time/ tasks management
- you have not been keeping up with your exercising routine
- you have not felt very motivated about the whole thing therefore you might need to review the reason why you chose to reach your perfect weight

Your awareness that something needs to be done differently, this time around, when the occasion presents itself, is what will make the difference in your results. Of course, the actions you take will also influence your results greatly. The opposite is true when we keep doing the same thing over and over again. In this case, there will be no change until we have learned the lessons and become aware of what needs to be changed.

When you fall forward it is with the understanding that what you are going through is only temporary and is part of your learning experience. However, this setback is not detrimental to your success or entire winning experience but rather instrumental in helping you do better next time.

"Failure is the key to success; each mistake teaches us something." - Morihei Ueshiba

Secret #3 to success in Everyday Life Balance™: Be willing to fall forward

4. Return to the bottom line

"The Pursuit of Happyness" is based on Chris Gardner's autobiography. I like to use Chris Gardner's autobiography to demonstrate what it takes to become successful as well as the positive impacts of self-empowerment. Through sheer determination Chris Gardner rose from homelessness to self-made millionaire in high finance in the 1980s. His life story is not only one of transformation, courage and tenacity but also an inspiring one. What was instrumental in Chris Gardner's success and the pursuit of his dreams was that he never gave up on his WHY because his WHY was strong enough. He was a single father and he did not want to give up on life and despair because of his love and care for his son. He says: "I made up my mind as a young kid that when I had children they were going to know who their father is and that he isn't going anywhere" (Chrisgardnermedia.com). Today, Chris Gardner is an entrepreneur, author, speaker, philanthropist, and a single parent.

Exercise 6

You have made the decision to create more balance in your life.

What is your WHY? In other words, why do you want it? Why is it important to you?

What would it mean to you to improve your everyday life balance?

Your success in achieving everyday life balance will be determined by your ability to clarify your WHY and to keep it constantly in mind and heart. When your WHY is big enough you achieve your goals more readily for you are motivated, inspired and persistent.

It takes courage to create change in your life because it requires some efforts on your part. When you are willing to create change you no longer allow the things that got in the way of your equilibrium to affect your life anymore. However, when you need courage you might hesitate or procrastinate because you have forgotten your WHY; 'why you are doing that? why you are spending so much time and energy into that? etc.'

Therefore, keep your WHY in mind; why you have made the decision to create change and to achieve your desired outcome. Change does not always come easily and your ability to persevere will be tested.

As you return to the bottom line you give yourself permission to start from where you are and move toward where you want to be step by step.

"He who has a why to live for can bear almost any how."
– Friedrich Nietzsche

Secret #4 to success in Everyday Life Balance™: Return to the bottom line

5. Allow yourself to receive

Your life can become imbalanced when you lose sight of the middle way. Particularly, when you spend most of your time giving and you do not allow yourself to receive. You might not allow yourself to receive for two reasons: you believe it is selfish or you believe you are not worthy. As a consequence, you close your heart to receiving.

Have you ever observed people's reactions when they are being praised or they are receiving words of appreciation? In most cases they either shy away from the compliment or they attempt to lessen the importance of it by saying something like: "Oh I bought them very cheaply!" if they have been complimented on their beautiful shoes, or "It's nothing!" if they do a kind gesture for someone or "Don't worry, I can do it" if they actually need help but do not want to 'be a nuisance' or 'disturb.' It is important to allow yourself to receive just because an open and loving heart is one which is opened to both giving and receiving. When you do not allow yourself to receive a compliment it means that you dismissed completely what the other person has praised you for from the bottom of their heart. You might say: "Oh but it is fake, it is not heartfelt." Could it be that it is not heartfelt because your heart is not open enough to receive? You must allow yourself to receive gracefully.

If you have the tendency to give a lot naturally you must open your heart to receiving also. This is true as much in your relationship with others, with yourself as it is with your Creator.

Exercise 7

You can do the following exercise by Joshua Bloom which is a great way to open your heart to receiving. This exercise is very energizing too:

Just stand up and close your eyes for a moment and visualize the rays of the sun or a golden light permeating your entire body. As you breathe in imagine that light reaching your feet and as you breathe out penetrating the earth. Repeat this breathing exercise ten times. As you do so you allow yourself to receive and experience your source of love. How do you feel?

"A closed heart is one which denies itself happiness."
– Pascale D. Gibon

Secret #5 to success in Everyday Life Balance™: Allow yourself to receive

6. Know that you are worthy

When you recognize in others their divine nature you recognize their worthiness. I recognize your worthiness, your inner beauty, and your inner diamond.

Magic happens when you allow:

♥ your inner diamond to shine

♥ your voice to be heard

♥ your truth to be expressed

There might be times when you stop yourself from having the things you truly desire, or doing the things you truly want just because you believe and feel that you are not worthy. Your mental activity might be: "I am not good enough to be this or to have that," "This person is better than me" etc. With such a low opinion of yourself you sabotage your own success.

Magic happens when you discover that you must allow your inner diamond to shine to its brightest. Your inner diamond is your worthiness and what you are here on earth to do. What are your gifts to the world? It could be as simple as the gift of giving, the gift of listening, the gift of smiling or the gift of making other people laugh. How you show up in life and how you honour your inner truth will determine your results.

When you show up as someone who is determined to give the best of you by allowing your inner diamond to shine you are a gift to the world.

Who are you not to let your inner diamond shine? When it does not shine you do a disservice to the world.

I remember Marion's story. She has been a wellness coach for many years and her dream was to become a professional speaker. Her ambition was to write a book in order to further her career. It took her 40 years to get her book done. She finally allowed her inner diamond to shine fully by letting her voice be heard through her book. By being an author, she was now able to pursue her professional speaking career very successfully.

I am sure that you have noticed in the previous chapters I use the word 'allow' when I intend for you to bring change in your life. From this place of 'allowing,' I am now going to discuss the law of acceptance in the next chapter.

"Let your inner diamond shine Bright Shining Star."
– Pascale D. Gibon

Secret #6 to success in Everyday Life Balance™: Know that you are worthy

CHAPTER 5

The Law of Acceptance

1. Everything is in perfect divine order

In order to alleviate stress and remain in the state of inner peace and well-being, it is important to remember that everything in life is in perfect divine order.

I spent a week in Spain back in April 2010 and I found myself stranded for four days due to the volcanic eruption in Iceland. So many people panicked in this situation, they were all eager to get home no matter what. Even if it took them four days to get there, through thick and thin they just wanted to get home.

I decided to respond calmly to the situation by putting my trust in God. Instead of reacting by getting stressed out I told myself: "Since I am in Spain and there is a Feria in Seville I am delighted to be here and to be able to spend extra days in the city." I am glad I did, this, was one of the most exciting experiences. Remember that the way we react or respond to things determine our results. It appears that I managed to fly back to England three days after the original date. I arrived at Seville airport expecting chaos, however, everything was normal, the airport was fairly empty and there were free seats at the back of the plane. I figured out that many people made their way to the closest port or Paris to get back to England, it must have been chaotic there and stressful!

You may have the tendency to put a lot of pressure on yourself, however, know that everything in life is in perfect divine order. With this awareness, it is then easier to deal with what might seem like setbacks and challenges.

Claire was very hard on herself, to such an extent that this was causing her worry and anxiety. I asked her:

When is good good enough?

Is it possible for you to be kinder to yourself?

From this moment on it was as if a whole load had been taken off her shoulders.

Perfectionism can paralyse us because it can stop us from moving forward and from getting anything done at all. The underlying feeling is one of fear, either the fear of failure or the fear of success. We fear being judged or we fear being praised.

If you are a perfectionist, consider how looking for imperfections might paralyse you and stop you from doing what you want to do.

People who are aware of the no-lose decision process know that mistakes can be corrected and that what is needed is to decide and to choose the path that seems most appropriate.

If there were no night, we would not appreciate the day, nor could we see the stars and the vastness of the heavens. We must partake of the bitter with the sweet. There is a divine purpose in the adversities we encounter every day. They prepare, they purge, they purify, and thus they bless."
– James E. Faust

2. Allow yourself to learn from the lessons

When you accept any situation for what it is and you respond to it as opposed to reacting to it you find peace. Acceptance is living in the moment and such reasoning brings you back to a sense of peace. The greater your acceptance the more you realize that the situation you might find yourself in is not outside of you, you have created it.

Someone may have done you wrong, misjudged you or criticized you, or simply hurt you. How you accept and perceive their behaviour will determine the outcome. The way you respond or react to the situation will be determined by your attitude. Your attitude combines your thoughts, feelings, and actions.

♥ Do you encourage peace or do you remain angry and bitter?

When an issue in your life repeats itself over and over again it is usually because there is still a lesson for you to learn. It is when you call upon and apply your own wisdom that the lesson is fully learned and a new lesson presents itself.

♥ What issue in your life presents itself over and over again and contributes to stress, disharmony, and imbalance?

You may react angrily, be resentful or revengeful even or you may respond by thinking: "This too shall pass!" Adjia was having a confrontational encounter with an acquaintance. She often runs away from the situation because she does not want to show her anger and frustration. She wondered, however, whether she was running from the situation by not confronting it dead on.

I coached her and she realized that letting go altogether is a higher level of awareness and life mastery. The ego will try to be right by wanting to go into an argument. Arguing for the sake of arguing generally leads nowhere as it falls on death ears when both parties want to be right. In order to improve the communication, it is always desirable to consider the other person's viewpoint and to accept where they are coming from.

"The more clearly you understand yourself and your emotions, the more you become a lover of what is."
– Baruch Spinoza

3. Let go of resistance

When you wish to create change in your life it is important that you align yourself with the law of non-resistance. It seems that many people remain stuck on the road of resistance. The road of least resistance i.e. the road of peace seems to be a long distance away. When we resist change we choose to be in disharmony with who we truly are and what really makes us happy. Your resistance comes from your paradigms or your multitude of habits, beliefs, and practices.

When you desire to change you resist it for fear of being disappointed and fear of the unknown. You do not know whether you will be better off or worse off. Thus, you apply the law of resistance: you want to change but you resist, resist, resist and you wrongfully believe that by resisting you will create change. As a result, you go round and round in circles and the stressful situation persists. No matter how much you want to change there remains disharmony between your thought and your true feelings and emotions. You are thinking one thing on the one hand and feeling another on the other hand.

In addition, you are resisting because you are not 100% sure of what you want. Another cause of resistance is your inability to make a committed decision because you have not made your mind up.

You align yourself with the law of non-resistance when you remove from your subconscious what you do not want and focus instead on what you really want. The most empowering tool at your disposal to let go of feelings and emotions held in your subconscious is the Sedona Method or the Release Technique. Lester Levenson founder of this technique said the following: "The Release Technique is based on the premise that each one of us has no limits except those that we hold onto subconsciously, and when we let go of our subconscious limitations, we discover that our potential is unlimited. Unlimited in the direction of health, happiness, affluence and materiality."

"Resistance as a means of securing peace and harmony is a mistaken and misleading idea. True harmony cannot come from in-harmony, nor peace from discord. Resistance fails because it is not in accord with harmony and order, which is the Law."
– Raymond Holliwell

4. Accept the best

It is when you accept the best in full faith that miracles happen. There are countless miracles happening throughout the world today. Believe in miracles by manifesting and acting upon what you truly desire.

You might deny yourself happiness because you feel that you are not worthy. It is necessary that you start deepening in your heart the thought and the feeling of being worthy, that it is possible to live a more peaceful and balanced life, to feel whole and complete. You hear often that gurus reach a state of bliss, it is simply the awareness that to allow yourself to experience joy and bliss you must reach a state of peace within and experience your true self. Like Dr. Wayne Dyer said: "Begin to see yourself as a soul with a body rather than a body with a soul." Once you accept this belief you understand that there is nothing to fear or doubt. Life is simply flowing as it should at this moment.

In order to accept the best your heart must be wide open to receiving. In chapter 4 I talked about how we shy away from real compliments when they are communicated to us. You must accept God's gifts as miraculous blessings. It is when you are balanced and happy that you can make a positive contribution to others happiness and give back.

> *There is a fundraising event in the UK called Red Nose Day or Comic Relief ('a just world free from poverty'), which was* first *launched in 1988. Every two years Comic Relief expect to surpass the money they raised the previous years from the generous public in order to help their chosen charities in the UK and Africa. You can be sure that year after year the amount raised goes up and up and up. They have high expectations and they know that the more they raise the more they can make a difference.*

In *Working with the Law,* Raymond Holliwell says: "Your expectation must be built up with your interest and attention." In the case of Comic Relief, when you look at their history they have innovated the concept over and over again by bringing in new ideas like Sports Relief and running special campaigns to raise even more money.

"Great sculptors and artists spend countless hours perfecting their talents. They don't pick up a chisel or a brush and palette, expecting immediate perfection. They understand that they will make many errors as they learn, but they start with the basics, the key fundamentals first."
– Joseph B. Wirthlin

5. How do you accept what is?

When you stop to worry and accept your situation for what it is, your whole perception of that situation changes; you become solution-focused as opposed to problem-focused. When you accept what is you dissipate any possibility of conflict and choose harmony instead. You have mastered the ability to respond vs. react. When you are with anger, for example, it is very difficult to see a situation clearly; however, when you choose inner peace and harmony, it is easier to let go.

You can ask your higher self for guidance: "What is the blessing and lesson this situation brings so that I can learn from it and move forward?" The more you accept what is, the more you allow yourself to let go and expand in awareness.

Free your mind by adopting a carefree attitude.

When we consider the life of Nelson Mandela, 'accepting what is' meant making sacrifices by giving up something of a lower nature (apartheid) in order to realize something of a higher nature (freedom). Nelson Mandela had a great mission and he had a bigger picture in mind: equality as the basis of human rights. It did not matter how much sacrifice was required as long as the long-term goal was achieved, which was to liberate his country. 'Accepting what is' also helped him grow in wisdom. In his mind nothing was greater than freedom no matter the price. He knew deep in his heart that time would be the greater healer.

To 'accept what is' requires great faith and the understanding that by law no matter what things will always get better.

"The keys to patience are acceptance and faith. Accept things as they are, and look realistically at the world around you. Have faith in yourself and in the direction you have chosen."
– Ralph Marston

6. Be happy!

In order to achieve everyday balance your belief in happiness must be strong. It requires that you play an active role in the creative process of your own happiness. A plant needs water to grow and to survive and as spiritual beings we also need to grow in awareness in order to live a life of fulfilment. Positive change can only occur through the creative process and falling in love with the idea that you are happy already. Therefore, in order to be happy your task is to be consciously engaged in the process of creation, transformation and progress.

The Creative Process of Happiness™ formula is a three-step formula. It entails that you connect to the spiritual side of you and write a new programme for the mind. Your mind is the greatest power in all creation. The reason why you are not happy is partly due to what is going on in your mind. By gaining a greater understanding of your thought process and beliefs you can transform your life and be happy.

This concept may appear simple to you because we underestimate the power of our mind and thoughts. What is going on inside shows on the outside. As you become more aware of your thought pattern and the vibration you are in (a negative or a positive one), you can create change in your life and be happier.

Exercise 8

In order to attain greater life balance:

Connect to your truth and be honest with yourself.

Co-create with your Higher Self the balanced life that you want.

Cultivate a way of being which is in harmony with your goal.

"If you want to see a happier world be happy."
– Mahatma Gandhi

PART TWO

CHAPTER 6

Being in the Now

1. Let go of the past

Before I go on let me first clarify some of the most important points I have made in the book so far.

- In order to live a more balanced life you made the decision to commit to transformation by looking within and by following the road of least resistance.
- You have learned the secrets to your success in achieving your goal.
- What leads to freedom and happiness is the acceptance and adoption of a new carefree attitude to life.

In the following chapters I am going to cover further your new attitude to life and reveal to you the Three Step Process for Everyday Life Balance™.

Suffering often occurs when you fear the past so much that you ignore the present and future. This will have negative influences on your everyday life balance. Here are some examples:

- you feel drained
- you are not able to see the situation clearly

- ♥ you are not experiencing the present moment for what it is
- ♥ you lack energy
- ♥ you feel disempowered
- ♥ you have low self-esteem
- ♥ you are bitter
- ♥ you are angry with yourself and others
- ♥ you are resentful
- ♥ you blame others
- ♥ you decrease your faith in life

Your life changes for the better when you take 100% responsibility for your life by acknowledging that there is a problem and correcting it by focusing on a solution.

> *Charlene went through three experiences where she felt let down by her partners in business. They made promises; however, they did not keep to their words. They drew a lovely picture of the business collaboration at the beginning yet the reality was something else. She felt undermined and exploited. As a consequence, she was full of mistrust. She lived in so much fear due to her past experiences that she let that fear interfere with her present life and paralyse her. She no longer knew who she could trust in business. She could not see her present life in a different light because she did not know how. Charlene* finally *acknowledged that she was making mistakes in business repeatedly and that she had to learn new business skills by hiring a business coach.*

It might be difficult for you to see a brighter future should you be firmly ingrained in the past and not allow change in your present.

What is past is past. Let it go; do not let it affect your present.

♥ Are you able and willing to draw a line on the past and create new positive circumstances?

"The knowledge of the past stays with us. To let go is to release the images and emotions, the grudges and fears, the clinging and disappointments of the past that bind our spirit."
– Jack Kornfield

2. Enjoy the present moment

Nothing brings you greater joy than when you are present in the now because you feel truly alive. I am grateful every day for a new day on what Master Ryuho Okawa calls: "the beautiful land of love, Earth." I always want to make the most of my day. I believe it is God's blessing and my desire is to honour this gift.

You can accept the present moment for what it is as you choose to be in total alignment with the flow of life and you allow yourself to just be and experience what is.

I always remind my personal development students to be fully present during a class so that they can make the most of their learning experience.

In today's fast-pace world it is increasingly difficult to be fully present. You will often see people being drawn to their mobile phone during a meal, when they are walking, when they are crossing the road, when they are in bed trying to sleep or when they are in the middle of a conversation for example.

The consequences of these new habits are that we are not fully present in the moment: we are not enjoying and savouring the food we are eating; we are not conscious of our environment; we are not actively listening when other people talk; our mind is active 24/7 and lastly, we are not quietening and resting our mind for a good night's sleep.

Do not dwell on the past; it no longer has a place in the present for you no longer live in the past. Do not live in the future but live in the now, the present moment; it is the decisions that you make and the seeds that you plant in the present moment, which will affect your future. The present is where your life is unfolding moment by moment. Be grateful for each day that passes. Be grateful for the breath of life. We are usually too concerned with tomorrow and forget to enjoy the present moment. Savour every present moment as if it was your last!

I sometimes hear people say: "I am glad it is Friday" after a long week of work. This suggests to me that work is about looking forward to Friday because then it is the weekend. Such an attitude also denotes that they are not living in the present moment but in the future. They look forward to the weekend regardless of whatever happens in the present. It is a shame to waste our time thinking of what will be instead of thinking of what is right now.

♥ What happens between Monday and Friday?

You cannot change your past but you can change your present right now. You can engage your freewill in order to enjoy every present moment as if it was your last. Life is an adventure and a series of experiences you can enjoy when they are pleasant and you can learn from when they are unpleasant. However, when you focus on the goodness of life you get more of it!

Every moment counts. As I am writing this book I am enjoying the process and I am thinking of you my reader transforming your life day by day. I am visualizing that you are happy, peaceful and full of joy and my heart is filled with love for you. Life is what you make of it and what you make of it is entirely your choice. God has given you free will.

"The ability to be in the present moment is a major component of mental wellness."
– Abraham Maslow

3. Simplify your life

Now is your time to get rid of the cobwebs that are in the way of your everyday life balance. It is for you time to:

♥ introduce new habits

♥ seek and find clarity

♥ declutter your mind of toxic thoughts that no longer serve you

♥ declutter your life of things that have become heavy baggage to carry, which are no longer useful in your life

♥ detach yourself from drama and other people's drama with compassion

♥ only allow space for what is important and not the superfluous or mundane

- deepen your understanding of what is
- know the truth
- change the way you look at things with compassion for others and yourself
- live from a place of acceptance and refuse to be upset or constrained by your circumstances
- become more resourceful

John is a very successful entrepreneur. He had a chain of restaurants. He had a lot of money; however, he was working 12 hours a day. His working habits created so much imbalance in his life that they affected his health and well-being. He fell into depression and he questioned the meaning of life: "I have all of the material things, brand new cars, a big house, expensive watches etc. yet I am unhappy." All the things he had were external, deep down he had not found his purpose. Everything in his life changed when a friend of his suggested he travelled to Africa with her to work in an orphanage. He said yes and his life has had more meaning since. He has now created his own humanitarian foundation.

When you detach yourself from other people's drama you are then able to see the situation clearly. You seek solutions and thus you can assist them the best way possible. John's friend saw clearly what was happening and she was then able to help.

When you simplify your life, you choose to travel 'baggage free.' Remember that life is as complicated as you want it to be. In truth, life is simple. In John's case he decided to stop working himself to the ground.

Remember that every single step that you take in the direction of greater life balance and well-being brings you closer to happiness.

"Simplicity is the ultimate sophistication."
– Leonardo da Vinci

4. Embrace joy

It is Monday morning and the beginning of the workweek. As I am sitting on the tube I am watching people's faces and expressions. Some faces are lit up others are not. I am having an internal monologue as I remember the cultural phenomenon called 'Monday Blues':

- ♥ Are they happy to be alive?
- ♥ Are they happy to be going to work?
- ♥ Are they probably tired?
- ♥ Did they have a busy weekend?
- ♥ Is something on their mind?
- ♥ Is work so boring?

The 'Monday Blues' has been described by Forbes as: "The start of the workweek triggering overwhelming feelings of anxiety, sadness, stress, lack of passion or motivation, sluggishness or tension."

Should you have fallen 'victim' of the 'Monday Blues' and love your job regardless here is an example of how you could beat it.

Julie likes her work; however, she asked me how she could be happier at work. I coached her on how she could change her attitude of mind in relation to work. As you wake up in the morning fill your mind with the intention to serve others throughout the day - serve your employer, your colleagues and your clients. Fill your mind with gratitude for the current job that you have been given to serve others. When you fill your day effectively and efficiently with gratitude and servitude you will be surprised by how much joy you gain from your work.

The mood you are in from the start of the day will have a ripple effect on the rest of your day. It is important that you wake up with joy because this is your true nature. When your thoughts resonate at a higher vibration you attract positivity in your life. Make it a habit that your thoughts resonate at a higher level of vibration by adopting positive thoughts.

"We are shaped by our thoughts; we become what we think. When the mind is pure, joy follows like a shadow that never leaves."
– Buddha

5. Mindfulness

In *The Mindfulness Solution* Ronald D. Siegel gives the following working definition of mindfulness: "Awareness of present experience with acceptance."

You might be mindful naturally without knowing or you might be mindless if for example you:

- ♥ are multi-tasking
- ♥ check your mobile while you are having lunch or dinner

- listen to someone in one ear and do something else
- get easily distracted
- you have a short attention span

It takes some practice to be fully grounded in the present moment by moment.

Julian is a friend of mine who has made the choice to be fully present in his life. When you talk to him you feel that he is truly listening, and connecting with you from a place of love. His only thought is one of paying full attention and being fully present without distraction. His main focus is his immediate experience. When he knows he has to move onto something else he would first finish his conversation with you then move on to his next task.

For everyday life balance it is necessary that you become a better observer and more aware of the present moment. Mindfulness is an approach to life which is based on the ability of observation.

This is what you could practise now:

Exercise 9

Coming from a place of silence you can observe your thoughts, feelings, sensations, breathing, body and your experience moment by moment. As you follow this process, you are fully awake in your own life; you pay attention with intention and without judgment, condemnation or self- criticism.

Mindfulness translates as holding the moment in awareness. Just embrace what is happening in this moment of silence, self-reflection and stillness. It puts you in touch with being as opposed to doing. It accesses your own powerful inner resources for insight, transformation and healing.

"The present is the only time that any of us have to be alive - to know anything - to perceive - to learn - to act - to change - to heal."
– Kabat-Zinn

6. Embrace life fully

You can allow yourself to have a complete experience here on earth and to play the game of life fully.

♥ When you are challenged you know how to respond.

♥ When you experience joy, you know how to embrace it.

Here is how the author Nadège Richards embraces life:

"I'm not sure I'll ever know the meaning of life or what comes for us after death, but I know it's more than the hysteria people make it out to be. It's about freeing your soul when no one else can; turning thirty and still feeling like you're seventeen. It's about taking chances on a whim, embracing the rain during the storm, and smiling so damn much that you start to cry. It's never regretting, never forgetting, and always being.

It's kissing underwater and touching in the dark. Loving even when you think it's emotionally impossible and surviving someway and somehow.

It's about living life with a full heart and an overflowing glass.

I live life on the edge. I dream, I care, and I belong. I know there's a here and now.

I know that I want it."

Celebrate life! The celebration of life is threefold: celebrate your uniqueness and your gift to the world; celebrate the present moment and lastly celebrate the fact that we are all one. For the purpose of living a more fulfilling and balanced life value the beauty of life and what is important to you.

"Today I choose life. Every morning when I wake up I can choose joy, happiness, negativity, pain... To feel the freedom that comes from being able to continue to make mistakes and choices - today I choose to feel life, not to deny my humanity but embrace it."
– Kevin Aucoin

CHAPTER 7

Improve Your Mind Power

1. You become what you think about

When you become aware of the three parts of your personality as a human being you gain a greater understanding of your power of creation, which you could utilize to create a new reality on a daily basis.

As illustrated by the stick person below, there are three parts to human personality:

- the conscious mind
- the subconscious mind
- the body

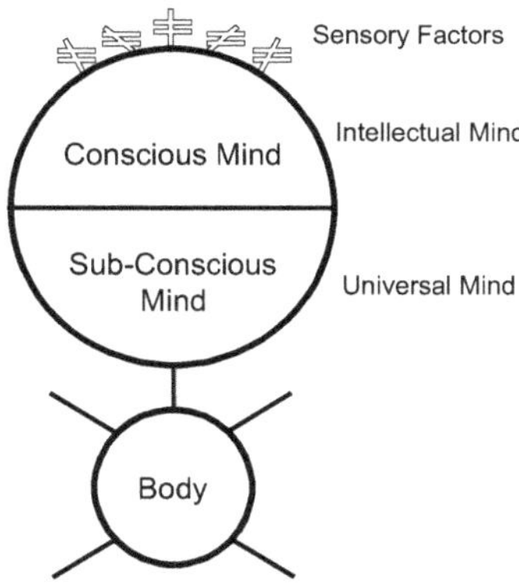

The concept of the stick person is the brainchild of Dr. Thurman Fleet a healer and chiropractor.

The mind is divided into two parts: the conscious mind and the subconscious mind.

The conscious mind is also known as the thinking mind, it is your reason, your free will, and your awareness. In your conscious mind you can choose your thoughts. You can choose anything you want or you can allow other people to choose them for you. The conscious mind has the ability to accept, reject, or neglect any thought.

The subconscious mind is also known as the feeling mind or the emotional mind. The subconscious mind stores your memories, life experiences, and paradigms. It can only accept the thought that is being impressed upon it for a long period of time.

The body is only an expression of your mind and the lower side of your nature, since everything begins in the form of thoughts. Therefore, the body moves your thoughts into actions.

To summarize, in your conscious mind you can choose your thoughts or you can allow other people to choose them for you. The thoughts you choose are expressed as feelings in your subconscious mind. These feelings produce actions, which produce results. Therefore, if you want to change your results, i.e. find balance in your life, you need to change what is going on in the inside first. You must be willing to change your thoughts.

Exercise 10

In this light, take a moment to reflect and become the observer of your life. Look at your current results and start drawing your balanced life on a blank canvas if you are not getting your desired outcome. The painter Van Goth said: "I dream my painting and I paint my dream."

"A man is literally what he thinks, his character being the complete sum of all his thoughts."
– James Allen

2. Keep your thoughts positive

Over the last 6000 years, scientists, philosophers, theologians, industrialists and capitalists agreed upon one thing: 'We literally become what we think about.'

Thus, you are free to choose thought impulses of a negative or destructive nature or of a positive or constructive nature. 'I cannot handle it! or 'I can do this!.' Whatever thought you choose to focus on the positive or the negative will determine your results.

In order to find balance in your life it is clear that a mind which entertains positive thoughts will help you reach the results you wish.

In his book *The Hidden Messages in Water,* Masaru Emoto's water crystal experiments reveal the effects of positive thinking on water. He concludes in his extensive research and discovery that water is closely related to our individual and collective consciousness and affirms:

"We all learn valuable life lessons at our own pace, but there is one basic truth we all learn early. Positive, compassionate words comfort and heal; negative words and insults hurt. Until recently, we knew this only because we could feel it. Now we can actually see it. Thanks to the experimental work of Dr. Masaru Emoto, we can look to water, and its frozen crystals, to confirm the healing power of beautiful music, positive thinking, uplifting speech, and prayer."

Additionally, according to Positive Psychology's scientific study, one of the pillars of well-being is positive emotion.

Winston Churchill said: "The pessimist sees difficulty in every opportunity. The optimist sees the opportunity in every difficulty." Therefore, if you have the tendency to be pessimistic, now is your time to become optimistic by seeing the opportunity in the difficulty you might be facing. The opportunity which presents itself might be one for change.

Claudia's dream is to be able to sing. She said: "I would love to sing however I cannot sing at all and it is just a dream." My response to her statement focused on how she could sing. My intention was to open her field of possibilities so I asked her: "In order for you to sing confidently would it be possible for you to learn the singing techniques and start by taking some lessons?" Her face lit up. I opened her up to the opportunity for greater life fulfilment. She can now choose to follow up on this new possibility by acting upon it.

"Happiness is not a matter of intensity but of balance and order and rhythm and harmony."
– Thomas Merton

3. The 3 'Ms' Formula of Everyday Life Balance™ – Master your mind

The 3 'Ms' Formula of Everyday Life Balance™ will help you to create order in your mind. As you follow this formula you will gain greater clarity, you will be more focused and less anxious or worried. The 3 'Ms' are identified as Master, Manage, and Monitor.

Step #1: Master your mind

You can reset your mind by increasing your ability to think in a way that serves you for your highest good. That is, by keeping your thoughts positive.

A client of mine, Kate, who attended my 'Yes! To Love' workshop followed this formula with great success. She had goals and ambitions however her mindset was not congruent with her dreams. When she started to review her thinking by entertaining more positive thoughts her self-belief increased as well as the belief that she could achieve her dreams. This first process alone created transformation in her life as she grew in awareness. With the right mindset, i.e. a mindset, that was in alignment with what she wanted, she was able to take action and follow her dreams.

You are congruent and able to get results when your thoughts, feelings and actions are in total alignment; this is called praxis. Any misalignment will make it very difficult for you to reach positive results fast. Let me give you an example:

- ♥ Your intention/want/wish: "I want more balance in my life"
- ♥ Your mindset: "I don't know if I am able to do it"
- ♥ Your actions: you will not take action toward your goal because of fear and doubt
- ♥ Your result: you remain stuck

You can empower yourself by practising the following positive and creative thinking process:

- ♥ Your intention/want/wish: "I want more balance in my life"
- ♥ Your mindset: "How can I do it?"
- ♥ Your actions: by law solutions will come to you because of your creative insight.
- ♥ Your result: as you put energy into achieving more balance in your life by taking actions, by law you will succeed.

"He who knows others is wise.
He who knows himself is enlightened."
– Lao Tzu

4. The 3 'Ms' Formula of Everyday Life Balance™ - Manage your activities

Step #2: Manage your activities

In order to create greater balance in your life you do not only manage your time you manage your activities also. Once you have identified your goals prioritize the steps you will need to take to move you in the direction of your goals and put aside any distraction. What you put energy in grows, therefore:

- ♥ What do you need to focus on more?
- ♥ What do you need to do right now to move in the direction of your goals?
- ♥ What do you need to do right now to help you get the results you want?

♥ What do you need to let go of?

This way of thinking will bring more structure and focus into your life. We can easily get distracted by the unnecessary, which inevitably slows our progress. Like Stephen Covey said, start scheduling your priorities right now.

♥ How could you organize your day better?

♥ What do you have to do less of?

♥ What do you need to do more of?

You can set up a list of about three to six daily tasks. You must assign a time to each task in order to ensure that you have a productive day in a balanced and orderly manner. You are not multi-tasking since you are focusing your energy on each task within a given time frame. This activity will also help you beat procrastination for you are assigning a time to each task.

> As you know, being an author requires a lot of discipline. By following the 3 'Ms' formula I had more balance on a daily basis and I was able to accomplish my goal of a completed book. My mindset was one of visualizing the end in mind, in other words I visualized myself holding the book *Yes! To Love*™ in my hand. 'Painting' my dream gave me the motivation to keep going and not procrastinate. As editing is the longest process, I needed to assign a time for editing purposes. I set myself the goal to edit at least one chapter a week. Because I gave myself a timeframe I was able to include this activity in my weekly schedule and to act upon it.

"The key is not to prioritize what's on your schedule, but to schedule your priorities."
– Stephen Covey

5. The 3 'Ms' Formula of Everyday Life Balance™ - Monitor your progress

Step #3: Monitor your progress

This last step in the 3 'Ms' formula is crucial. In order to see things more clearly and to move forward step by step, it is important that you monitor your progress. Additionally, when you monitor your progress you think into results. Some adjustments might be necessary therefore it is equally important to know where you are and how the new habits you have introduced are improving your results.

You have decided; you have chosen to create change in your life by having more balance.

- ♥ How well are you doing?
- ♥ Has anything changed for the better?
- ♥ Have you made any steady progress?
- ♥ Do you feel more balanced?
- ♥ Do you have greater inner peace?
- ♥ Do you feel calmer?
- ♥ Have you created more order in your life?
- ♥ Do you feel more in control of your life?
- ♥ Do you feel more confident?
- ♥ Do you feel more fulfilled?

- Are you able to handle better unforeseen situations?
- Do you feel more motivated?

If you are not getting the results you wish for please return to either step 1 or step 2 of the formula and take further actions.

- For example, if you are challenged at work and feel overwhelmed, it is better to tackle one thing at a time so that you can monitor your progress more efficiently and with greater clarity. There is no point in beating yourself up for not getting things done all at once! Like Abraham Lincoln said: "I am a slow walker, but I never walk back."

"Those who do not move, do not notice their chains."
– Rosa Luxemburg

6. Do the things you love and love the things you do

In order to identify and to align yourself with what makes your heart sing it is important that you reconnect to your passions. Your life flows and is in balance when you do the things you love, which are unique to you. It seems that we have more energy and we are more inspired, motivated, alive and fulfilled when we devote time to the things that are really important to us and which resonate with us.

- What do you love to do and be?

As a Passion Test Facilitator, I have done the Passion Test with a number of my personal development students. In most cases what they believe to be important to them is not necessarily what their heart truly desires in the first instance. You find the truth when you connect to your soul's desires. Indeed, when you are inspired you are truly in tune with your heart and what you love.

In order to find inner balance connect to your heart and find what truly moves you, resonates with you and what you would trade your life for.

Let me share with you Cynthia Kersey's inspirational story.

I met Cynthia in London in 2010 when she was in transit from Africa back to America. Cynthia is the author of the best-selling book "Unstoppable." Her passion is giving back so she made the conscious decision to devote more time to the people who need help the most and founded in 2008 The Unstoppable Foundation (www.unstoppablefoundation.org). This non-profit organization focuses on Sub-Saharan Africa and is committed to empowering lives through education and to bringing sustainability to people in developing nations. Their mission is to ensure that every child has access to the lifelong gift of education thereby building a thriving, just and sustainable world. To date her decision to create The Unstoppable Foundation has resulted in more than 29,667 lives being impacted positively.

Cynthia loves her philanthropic work, she cultivates the gift of giving every single day and she is very happy and fulfilled. This is her message and worthy ideal: "We will not stop until every child on the planet has access to education – we are unstoppable!".

"Passion arises from the heart, and your heart's impulse is more likely to be closer to the truth than your mind's analysis."
– Janet Bray Attwood, co-author of the Passion Test

CHAPTER 8

Uplift Your Body

1. Your body is your temple

Your body is beautiful you must honour it like a temple. Whatever nourishment you give it; it will respond with discomfort or ease. Care for every part of it.

Your body houses your spirit you can talk to anyone who has had a near death experience and they will confirm that it is so. Treat your body with reverence.

Your body is powerful and like Socrates said: "What a disgrace is for a man to grow old without ever seeing the beauty and strength of which his body is capable."

Be kind to your body it will always thank you for it. Connect to your body and when your life is imbalanced allow yourself some rest and adequate sleep; it is the best medicine. It is during resting and sleeping times that your body actually heals.

In the previous chapter, you discovered the three parts to human personality: the conscious mind, the subconscious mind and the body. The body is what puts into action what lies in the conscious and subconscious mind. Therefore, the body plays a pivotal role in ensuring that you realize what you wish to achieve by taking action. In this light, it is important that you remain in good health and full of vitality to create greater balance in your life.

The body knows best what optimizes its functionality and what does not. When you feel tired, for example, you could simply focus on reviewing your sleeping pattern in order to restore the body to its state of balance; you could introduce some exercise or even stretching if you are not doing so already. Let us look at other ways you could uplift your body.

"Take care of your body it is the only place you have to live."
– Jim Rohn

2. The importance of good nourishment

In addition to your psychological and emotional well-being you take care of your physical well-being by eating a healthy diet. It is in time of stress that one tends to under nourish or malnourish themselves. One generally goes for processed foods and takeaways instead and thus one loses control over what they nourish their body with.

It is very important that you nourish your body with micronutrient rich foods in order to function better and to increase your well-being. These micronutrients include foods which are rich in dietary fibre, vitamins and minerals. Allow these foods to become your natural medicine for the maintenance of good health.

Although *Yes! To Love*™ is not a book on nutrition, here are the building blocks of good nutrition:

Carbohydrates: they are vital for energy.

Proteins: they are essential for cell growth, tissue repair and reproduction and to protect against infection.

Lipids: also known as fats, they play an important role in your body such as providing energy, producing hormones, facilitating food absorption and digestion.

Vitamins: they are essential nutrients your body needs in small amounts. There are two types: fat-soluble and water soluble. They help the body work properly.

Minerals: they are necessary to build strong bones and teeth, to control body fluids and to turn the food you eat into energy.

According to the World Health Organization, by introducing Five a Day i.e. five portions of fruit and vegetables (minimum 400g) you achieve a balanced diet and this can help you stay healthy.

However, good nourishment does not only come from food. I cannot stress enough the importance of water to well-being on a daily basis. I often come across people who are tired because of dehydration: they have been on a long flight; they spend hours in front of the computer; they have been exercising and still feel very stiff; their lips are dry because they have not been drinking enough water. In fact, if you are a coffee drinker, for each caffeinated cup that you drink you ought to drink a glass of water due to the diuretic effects of caffeine.

In his book *The Body Many Cries for Water* the late Dr. F Batmanghelidj did extensive studies on the subject of chronic dehydration. He was imprisoned for two years in Iran and discovered that many of his inmates' complaints were due to dehydration. You might feel fatigued; however, your body might be crying for water. Dr. Batmanghelidj's recommended consumption of water is : 6 oz (1.2l) to 8 oz (1.9l) glasses per day minimum. He also mentions in his book that dry lips are in fact the last sign of dehydration. Additionally, staying hydrated for well-being does not include drinking coffee and tea as substitutes.

Lastly, keeping your immune system strong will help you counteract the effects of stress.

"Prevention is better than cure."
– Desiderius Erasmus

3. The importance of exercising

Exercising is sometimes the antidote to life imbalance as it re-energizes you and stimulates serotonin the hormone that creates the feel-good factor. However, the secret to regular exercise is to do one that motivates and stimulates you and that you really enjoy doing. As a result, exercise becomes an activity that gives you a lot of pleasure and makes you feel great.

Physical activity does not only include going to the gym but also horseback riding, gardening, walking, dancing, cycling etc.; whatever keeps you fit and moving. Your physical activity does not have to be intense either. I personally recommend stretching on a daily basis. Stretching has an amazing positive impact on the body it decreases muscle stiffness and increases your flexibility. Daily stretches do not take long if your time is limited. Walking instead of driving, walking up and down the stairs instead of using the escalators; these simple opportunities for physical activity count in creating everyday life balance.

I remember watching a documentary on the UK TV presenter and entertainer Bruce Forsyth whose career spanned 75 years. He revealed his secret for longevity, everlasting energy and health. At 87 he followed daily an ancient exercise regime favored by Tibetan monks. This exercise regime was laid out by the Tibetan monks more than 2,500 years ago. Bruce Forsyth got his inspiration from Peter Kelder's book "Eye of Revelation." Additionally, a healthy breakfast followed his exercise routine. This is how Bruce Forsyth increased his strength, longevity and flexibility.

Harriette Thompson, a concert pianist and cancer survivor, became the oldest woman to complete a marathon at the age of 92. She finished the San Diego Rock 'n' Roll marathon in 2015. Thompson said: "I feel if I can do it anybody can do it, because I wasn't trained to be a runner. But I have also found that it is very invigorating. I feel like a million dollars when I'm finished."

I have encountered many people who have improved their well-being simply by taking the time to include physical activity in their life. Exercise keeps your body in shape and your mind, body and spirit balanced!

You might find it easy to become demotivated; however, a regular exercise regime requires a level of self-discipline and you need therefore to include an exercise routine in your weekly schedule.

"Physical fitness is not only one of the most important keys to a healthy body, it is the basis of dynamic and creative intellectual activity."
– John F. Kennedy

4. Listen to your body

Science has proven that as you improve your mind power this will have a positive effect on your body. Science has shown that thoughts do not only affect your brain but also your organs.

As shown by the body work Rosen Method, which was founded by the physiotherapist Marion Rosen, by applying small pressure on any part of the body the client is able to reveal any pent-up emotion. This work is done alongside using the client's breath. I remember experiencing the Rosen Method and I was amazed by the emotional release I encountered during the treatment. As I lay on the massage table I went back as far as 12 years old, remembering particular events that have had a real impact on me. I was still holding the emotions related to these events in my subconscious mind and they manifested themselves in my body.

I am fortunate enough to do Chris James' ultimate internal cleanse every year called '12 days'. As I listen to my body I know when it is time for me to do the cleanse. It is a symbiosis between clearing my body of toxins for greater physical performance and well-being and clearing my mind of toxic thoughts for greater clarity.

Signs of stress can manifest themselves in very subtle ways; therefore, you must become aware of the signs:

♥ feeling tearful for no reason

♥ feeling tired mentally and physically

♥ feeling lethargic

♥ insomnia

♥ feeling edgy, irritable, impatient

♥ low energy

♥ pain in your stomach

- ♥ frequent colds and infections
- ♥ loss of libido
- ♥ muscular aches and pains

Once you know the sign it is time to rest and return to a state of balance.

"Your body speaks to you it is up to you to listen."
– Pascale D. Gibon

5. Yoga and meditation

I have been practising yoga and meditation for many years. I mainly practise Hatha yoga which is part of Raja yoga (the science of physical and mental control). Yoga means union, humility, tolerance, restraint, calm and detachment. This Eastern tradition dates back to at least 3000BC. What I love about yoga is the balance it creates between 'doing' and 'being' using the breath. I often use yogic breathing for healing and de-stressing.

The breath of life is instrumental in creating balance when you are overwhelmed or stressed out: as you breathe deeply through your nose and slowly through your mouth (through your nose if you practise yoga) you inhale oxygen and expel carbon dioxide, water vapour, alcohol vapours and any other toxic gases. If you are a shallow breather, I recommend you train yourself to breathe more deeply. As part of your everyday life balance when 'the going gets tough' just take a deep breath with the aim to find inner peace again.

The beauty of yoga is the ability to practise it without it being strenuous; yoga is more than physical exercises. It is the ability to reach the stage where the asana (posture) and the breath are totally in sync as one. This comes with practice. Additionally, your yoga practice becomes effortless when you adopt the attitude of letting the breath lead the movement and not the other way round.

There is relaxation in yoga called shavasana and it is my favourite moment in a yoga practice. At this particular moment, you lie on your back and you let go of any tension you may be holding in your body using your breath and focusing on your third eye. This is the moment when you truly allow yourself to let go and to just be. During this relaxing time everything gets connected your mind, body and spirit. Its meditative quality lies in the ability to purely focus on the breath and to let go of any thought.

The aim of meditation is to calm the mind by becoming an observer of your thoughts and by detaching yourself from them. This results in a great sense of inner peace and oneness with your true self. Many of my students say that they have tried to meditate, but they cannot stop themselves from thinking. The good news is that you cannot stop the mind from thinking; however, with practice you can learn to let go of your thoughts, to become an observer and to find yourself in a state of total stillness and bliss.

The practice of yoga and meditation will not only increase your flexibility, slow the ageing process and reconnect you to the breath it will also create greater everyday life balance as it promotes well-being at every level.

> ***"The art of breathing or 'pranayama' (prana means 'life force or energy' while yama means 'regulation of') is an integral part of yoga practice. By controlling your breathing, you can increase your stamina, boost your general well-being and improve your energy levels, alertness, and clarity of mind. Breathing is therefore one of the most effective and economical ways of treating ill health."***
> ***– Dr. Ali***

6. Keeping in balance

As the saying goes, 'everything in moderation.' For example, you know you have not been eating properly for a while, or that you have overindulged, you can counterbalance these excessive habits with healthy eating habits and increase your exercise regime.

To keep everything in balance you must become aware of the following symptoms of stress:

- ♥ **Some physical symptoms**: tension headache; jaw and teeth are clenched; shoulder tension; back pain; rapid, shallow breathing; heart racing and palpitations; mouth dries up; eyes strain; abdominal pain, skin problems; perspiration increases; bladder relaxes; blood vessels close; skin tightens; menstrual problems in women; impotence and premature ejaculation in men.
- ♥ **Some emotional symptoms**: anxiety, irritability; anger; depression; mood swings; hopelessness and increased addictive behaviour.
- ♥ **Some mental problems**: poor concentration; lack of confidence; mental sluggishness; lack of discrimination; poor

memory; poor decision-making; reluctance to change; poor attention span and panic attacks.

I believe that the part of your body that you must keep healthy is the core of your body, your abdomen. This is where you hold most of your emotions: 'you have a gut feeling,' 'you feel like emptying your bowels.' The best way to strengthen this part of the body is through Pilates, Yoga, body strengthening, balancing classes, sit ups or press ups or chakra healing. Doreen Virtue calls it the solar plexus or third chakra. It is your power house, the energy centre which corresponds to your self-empowerment. Any imbalance in this area will undermine your level of self-confidence. I recommend chakra healing to anyone who wishes to heal, rebalance and re-energize their energy centres, their chakras. Chakra is a Sanskrit term which translates as wheel or disk. In yoga, meditation and Ayurveda it relates to the wheels of energy throughout the body. The 7 main chakras align the spines, starting from the base of the spine through to the crown of the head. However, there are chakras throughout the body. Their functions within the human body are to help regulate all its processes, from organ function to the immune system and emotions.

"Balance – The ultimate goal"
– Ricky Lankford

Bonus #3
Uplift Your Body & Mind

Get the audio recording with Chris James founder of Chris James Mind Body free at:

http://www.yestolovebook.com

CHAPTER 9

Uplift Your Spirit

1. You are 100% responsible for your life

How you respond to a particular situation is entirely up to you, and this will affect the way you feel about it. For example, someone has done you wrong and you might resent them. This feeling of resentment stays with you for a long time because you are still blaming the person who hurt you and you are still bound emotionally to an event that happened in the past. The other person, on the other hand, has moved on and forgotten about it. You are still holding a grudge. Since it is how you choose to respond to the situation that counts, you have to take full responsibility for your own feelings. Another resort would be to simply decide to severe the cord that binds you to this person by choosing to let go and forgive.

Since our life is a workbook of problems that need to be solved, you must accept that whatever happens in your life is intended as part of your personal growth. Without your workbook of problems there would be no room for you to grow and become a better person.

Responsibility is your ability to respond. Out of the 7 Levels of Awareness, the ability to respond versus react is the top level, the level of mastery. Thus, how you respond to your life and to your workbook of problems will determine the type of life you experience.

Should you be someone who blames others for your work-book of problems, you can now make the commitment to take full responsibility for your life.

"Man must cease attributing his problems to his environment and learn again to exercise his will – his personal responsibility."
– Albert Einstein

2. Become carefree

The saying goes, 'Que sera sera!'; 'What will be will be!' In other words, to free yourself of any worry it is always best to release it to the universe in good faith.

One of my cousins had an interview as a postdoctoral researcher and she was so stressed out and worried about it that she started to panic by feeling physically sick and unable to control her fear. In order to lighten her up I said to her: "Be carefree, do your best and release all worries to the universe. You know that the universe is always looking after you and that your guardian spirit is by your side always therefore there is nothing to fear. If the job is meant for you it will be yours."

She did feel relieved knowing that she was not alone and that she was fully supported in her endeavour. In fact, she really calmed down and she was then able to centre herself and regain equilibrium.

As part of the laws of the universe, the law of compensation stipulates that when a door closes something greater awaits you.

When your way of thinking is expansive, creative and positive, you find greater balance. When you are carefree you rid yourself of anything that would create an imbalance, like for example a negative mental activity or feeling. However, to be carefree does not mean to be careless but rather to be free and detached from unnecessary worries which create the imbalance in the first place. My cousin worked hard to prepare for her interview; therefore, she was more than ready.

When you become carefree you are also aware that you always strive to do your best whatever the circumstances may be. As you increase faith in yourself and in the Creator, you can allow yourself to let go of worries, fears and doubts that tend to impact your life excessively. As you become carefree you have faith and the belief that 'this too shall pass.' According to the law of rhythm when you are on a down swing, do not feel bad. Know and believe the swing will change and things will get better.

When a problem arises ask yourself the following questions:

♥ Does it really matter?

♥ Is it really important?

In most cases we blow problems out of proportion out of fear.

"We are not human beings having a spiritual experience. We are spiritual beings having a human experience."
– Teilhard de Chardin

3. Let go of attachments

When you are stressed you might have the tendency to see the worst. When you simplify your life, you choose to put aside anything that no longer seems significant to you by detaching yourself from it. According to Lester Levenson it is attachment that creates suffering.

For example, you are overwhelmed; you have just moved into a new house, you have to unpack, the house is a mess it needs cleaning, and you are close to tears because you do not know where to start. You could open yourself up to a new field of possibilities:

- ♥ You could choose to follow a step by step process which would simplify the whole scenario and would make it easier for you to handle.
- ♥ You could change your thought process whereby instead of thinking that you should do it all at once, which is overwhelming, you could choose to do it step by step. When you take baby steps you clean one room and once you see the results you will be more motivated to do the others.
- ♥ You could change your mindset whereby instead of thinking that you cannot handle it you ask yourself how you could be more in control.
- ♥ You could work on improving your organizational and prioritizing skills in order to operate more efficiently and productively.
- ♥ And lastly, you could become resourceful by asking for help or seeking the guidance of someone who has been there before.

Henry is a manager who would not let go of his work phone. He is so attached to his phone that he would not put it aside when he was asked to do so. When we met his reply was: "I have to hold my phone." He was having a break from work; however, he was still attached to his phone. He was waiting for the phone to ring at any moment and he was also expecting a message. Guess what?! His wishes were fulfilled. Henry received a number of messages during our consultation. Suddenly, he got up saying in a panic: "Oh no, sorry I have to go now. There are serious things happening at work." Janet Bray Attwood, author of "The Passion Test" comments: "What you put your attention on grows." Unfortunately, in Henry's case it seems that he put his attention on creating more stress for himself.

As you let go of attachments you become more and more carefree. Should you tend to overcomplicate things or to blow them out of proportion simplify your life by changing your thinking and your perception of what is.

"What we perceive to be problems in our lives are nothing to do with what is happening in the world and everything to do with the limitation of our mental maps."
–Michael Neill

4. Change your perception

We define perception as our point of view. When we look at life with spectacles other than the ones we have been conditioned by, we most certainly get a different picture. If the way you perceive your life now is that you are 'overwhelmed,' 'helpless' because nothing is working in your life, allow yourself to change this thought immediately. Firstly, something must be working; secondly there is always a spiritual solution. As stated by Raymond Holliwell you have the power to: "Master your mind and guide it intelligently: that is, exercise discrimination in all your thinking."

♥ What you thought impossible now becomes possible.

You must know that you have the answers within you for a more balanced life.

Byron Katie, creator of "The Work" process, estimates that: "We discover that all the concepts and judgments that we believe or take for granted are distortions of things as they really are. When we believe our thoughts instead of what is really true for us, we experience the kinds of emotional distress that we call suffering. Suffering is a natural alarm, warning us that we're attaching to a thought; when we don't listen we come to accept this suffering as an inevitable part of life. It's not."

It is through the daily practice of prayer, meditation and exercise that I re-energize and I find my equilibrium. This is how I reconnect with my Higher Power.

You must find your own way of finding inner peace, may it be by engaging in activities such as:

♥ connecting with nature

♥ connecting with others

♥ reading an inspiring book

♥ entertaining positive thoughts

♥ painting, drawing or gardening

♥ creating a piece of music

♥ exercising etc.

What brings you the greatest sense of peace?

Whatever makes your spirit sing works, this is for you to discover.

"God loves you, surrender to his love by saying: Yes! to Love."
– Pascale D. Gibon

5. Replace fear by love

Do not let fear get in the way of love! You must let go of fear and replace it by love.

FEAR stands for Fantasized Experiences Appearing Real. You become a victim of fear when you allow fear to dominate your thinking and to paralyse you.

> For example, if you are an actor or a dancer going for an audition, before you even get there you beat yourself up with thoughts like: "What if they don't like me?" "What if I am not good enough?" "What if I don't fit the part?" etc. Before you even know it, you have set yourself up for failure because of your disempowering and limiting thoughts. On the contrary, empowering thoughts would help you set the right intentions; to get as far as you can, to do your best and eventually to get the part or the job.

Fear has a big role to play in the way we feel and act: "Fear seems to be epidemic in our society. We fear beginnings; we fear endings. We fear changing; we fear 'staying stuck.' We fear success; we fear failure. We fear living; we fear dying" says Susan Jeffers in her book *Feel the Fear and Do It Anyway*. It is clear that fear tends to dominate our world and can render us paralysed and helpless.

I remember having a conversation with a friend about her work situation. She was really happy to receive many work opportunities after many months without work and she was looking forward to reviving her career. However, she said something that puzzled me: "Wow, all these opportunities are great, but I do not want to get too excited in case they do not materialize." What she did was to let fear dominate her mind; why shouldn't she get excited? Why shouldn't she let her heart sing?

When you bring up fearful emotions you deny yourself the most important thing of all, Love. However, you can turn things around.

Exercise 11

Take a deep breath and think for a moment of a situation or a thought that troubles you, release the fear and replace it with love. You do this by having empowering thoughts and by becoming emotionally involved with thoughts of love. As you open your heart, allow love to penetrate your whole body and embrace love.

Could you change your fear to love? What happened? Do you feel relieved and lighter? Your energy field has in fact shifted from a lower vibration (fear) to a higher vibration (faith) because you entertained higher thoughts. Fear is associated with lower energy vibration.

Although in the 'fight or flight' response, fear is associated with a stimulus to act by fighting or flying, in most cases fear is associated with pain. The fear we should be more concerned about is the one that generates negative emotions constantly. In order to release the fear, to move away from pain and toward happiness, you can ask yourself the following two questions:

Exercise 12

1. Am I committed to myself and to my life?

2. Is there space in my life for more inner peace, more balance, more harmony, more love and more happiness?

Once you have made a decision, commit to it by taking action.

"The only remedy known for fear is understanding. When one understands that the universe is filled with the presence of God, there is nothing to fear."
– Raymond Holliwell

6. Enjoy life as a gift

When you adhere to the idea that life is a workbook of problems for growth, it then becomes easier to welcome life's challenges and to enjoy life as a gift.

There are things you are blessed with, thus now is the time to count your blessings.

♥ Begin by recognizing the goodness that exists in you and in your life.

♥ Honour the things you are blessed with.

♥ Be thankful every day from a place of appreciation for what you have been given.

The more grateful you are the more blessed you become.

♥ As you wake up in the morning, spell out five things you are truly grateful for in your life. Be grateful even for the simplest thing.

♥ When something great happens be grateful for that gift.

As a result, when you live your life at a higher level of consciousness you understand that the meaning of life is to live in harmony with your true spiritual nature: a being of light whose centre is pure love, joy, harmony, peace and abundance.

When everything you do in your life comes from this place of love, you are balanced and happy. This is the true nature of existence. When your life becomes the expression of pure and unconditional love, you no longer need to control anything for you are in the flow of life and in harmony with spirit. You are whole, perfect and complete when you allow yourself to give love and to receive love.

"Life is a gift and you are a gift to the world. It is up to you to exercise your free will in order to experience a magical life.
The choice is entirely yours."
– Pascale D. Gibon

CHAPTER 10

The Power of Love

1. A message of love

Love is the answer. When you seek everyday balance in your life you choose to transform your beingness into one of love. Moreover, your whole being is a reflection of love.

Love enables you to solve the many problems you may have. Love is your salvation. In order to live from the perspective of everyday life balance you open your heart to love more and more every day. As the day ends you may ask yourself whether you gave love today or took love.

Living from the perspective of love also means to reward yourself every day and to allow yourself to receive.

Love is peace. When you include more love in your daily life you find peace and balance.

When Nelson Mandela was imprisoned he chose peace. He declared: "I always knew that deep down in every human heart, there was mercy and generosity. No one is born hating another person because of the colour of his skin, or his background, or his religion. People must learn to hate, and if they can learn to hate, they can be taught to love, for love comes more naturally to the human heart than the opposite. Even in the grimmest times in prison, when my comrades and I were pushed to our limits, I would see a glimmer of humanity in one of the guards, perhaps just for a second, but it was enough to reassure me and keep me going. Men's goodness is a flame that can be hidden but never extinguished."

Love is gratitude. Remember to be grateful for all the goodness, which is in your life.

Let me share with you the story of the man who is stuck on the top of a roof and asks God for help. The story goes:

There once was a man trapped on the roof of his house while dangerous flood waters were rising up all round him. Clinging to the chimney, he feared for his life. Never before had he felt such a desire to live. He called for help, "Dear God, I want to live. Please help." Instantly God replied, "I will help you my Son."

Shortly thereafter, a neighbour came by in a canoe: "Hop in old boy," cried the neighbour. "Thanks anyway, but God is on His way," cried the man.

Time passed, and the flood waters still continued to rise. A complete stranger passed by in a motor boat and this Good Samaritan offered the man a lift. "Thanks anyway, but God is on His way," cried the man.

Soon the man was standing on top of his chimney, the waters still rising. Out of nowhere, a helicopter arrived with rope. "Thanks anyway, but God is on His way," cried the man.

The man eventually drowned. Before Heaven he angrily confronted God, "Why didn't You help me?" he cried. "I would have thought You of all people would have kept Your word."

"Well, I tried," said God, "I came in a canoe and motor boat and a helicopter, but each time you turned me away."

"Spread love everywhere you go.
Let no one ever come to you without leaving happier."
– Mother Teresa

2. Love is the answer

Like Socrates said: "Wear love everywhere you go." Open your heart to love. Do you remember Cynthia's story? She told me that out of all the things she has done setting up a charity to help education in Africa as well as communities has been the most rewarding thing ever. To this date, Cynthia is actively involved in raising money to further the education of the children in Africa.

What really happened? A life that seemed perfect from the outside was imbalanced according to Cynthia. She needed to reach out and dig deep into the core of her being to discover her core desires. By digging deep into her heart Cynthia was able to see a wider picture and spread her wings further. Love that stretches beyond one's personal needs helped her bring her life back into balance.

By now you will understand how important it is to open up your heart to the many gifts available to you. For example: we are always given the opportunity for growth, expansion, greater awareness, greater wisdom to give more love, to recognize the love we have been given, to forgive, to let go and to understand etc.

To put it simply by introducing love into your everyday life you will find everyday balance. Love yourself when you are too hard on yourself and love others. What is required of you is to recognize their suffering in the case of conflict for example.

In today's society we should put greater emphasis on love and compassion in order to create greater everyday life balance. A heart filled with love and wisdom creates a miraculous and harmonious life.

As you create harmony in your life through your increased capacity to love, this will have a positive impact on your immediate environment, your city, your country and the world at large.

"Life is so much easier when you're
in the feeling stream of love."
– Larry Crane

3. Love yourself

You know that your life is imbalanced; however, you cannot pinpoint why. If this is the case, most of the time, you have denied yourself the right to be worthy: to be worthy of love, to be worthy of receiving, to be worthy of a happier life, to be worthy of the many gifts that are available to you.

I come across many people who are real givers yet they are unable to receive. Everyday life balance means the ability to be able to both give and receive. If you give too much and you do not allow yourself to receive, your life is imbalanced and you might become resentful as a consequence. If you receive too much and do not give, your life is imbalanced and you have forgotten how much has been given to you; you have become a taker and dependent.

You are a gift to the world and you shying away from the expression of your uniqueness and from the world is a disservice to your greatness and to the many people who are part of your life right now. The greater your love for yourself, the greater your love for others. As you love yourself more others will reflect your greatness and you will inspire love.

I remember John's story. There were two brothers living with their single mother in a poor neighbourhood. Their dad left home when they were in their early teens. The two brothers reacted differently to their circumstances: one became very bitter and ended up in prison and the other became better and is now a motivational speaker. The latter made the choice not to become a victim of his circumstances and against all odds to create a better life for himself and his family. His determination, persistence and self-belief were so strong that he made it. The former simply gave up due to a lack of self-belief and lack of awareness that your circumstances do not dictate your future.

With regard to creating greater balance in your life always start from a place of love and determine whether you are being loving and loveable. It is true that when you are loving you are loveable and you are loved. When you are not loving enough it is time to look at ways you can clean the window of your heart and deepen your well of love.

"As I began to love myself I recognized that my mind can disturb me and it can make me sick. But as I connected it to my heart, my mind became a valuable ally. Today I call this connection WISDOM OF THE HEART."
– Charles Chaplin

4. Grow in compassion

Mother Teresa devoted her life to serving the poor and the destitute around the world. She spent many years in India, particularly in Calcutta, where she founded the Missionaries of

Charity. She said: "It is not how much we do, but how much love we put in the doing. It is not how much we give, but how much love we put in the giving."

The Oxford dictionary gives the following definition of compassion: a strong feeling of sympathy for people who are suffering and a desire to help them.

When you show compassion for others you create more balance in your life. Growing in compassion entails the ability to grow in love for others. We all have different values and beliefs therefore different ways of seeing things. It is almost always best to meet the other person half way if you disagree with them. It is not a question of saying you are right and I am wrong, but rather a question of meeting the other person half way by accepting their perspective as it is a reflection of their own reality and level of awareness.

If you are involved in a dispute, for example, your tendency might be to judge or criticize straight away. Any judgment or criticism will actually be reflected back to you. It is always best to use your wisdom and understanding that the other person is suffering more than you. As a consequence, you have just said Yes! to love as opposed to saying yes to hate, anger, disgust, and grudge for the rest of your life. The latter, carrying a negative resonance, will create discomfort and imbalance in your life. A simple step is to recognize in others their deepest fears and feel compassionate for we are all one.

When you envelop your entire being with love, pride has no place, nor does the desire to win at all cost. You show compassion and consideration when you help someone struggling with their luggage on the tube; when you open the door for someone who has their hands full; when you take the time to listen to someone who is clearly in pain; when you share your wisdom, your love and understanding for example.

"If you want others to be happy, practice compassion, if you want to be happy practice compassion."
–The Dalai Lama

5. The gift of tolerance

Tolerance is the ability to accept and to understand others better; therefore, it is also at the core of love. Showing more tolerance for others requires some effort on your part. It requires you to dig deep into your heart and view any challenging situation from a place of love. For example, you want someone to do something and what they do is not to your liking because they are not doing it your way. Some efforts on your part will be required; you will need to understand that we are all different in the way we do things. It is possible to show them a different way of doing things without imposing your way forcefully.

Similarly, if you have a particular opinion about something and your interlocutor completely disagrees, tolerance is required because they are entitled to their own opinion. Yours as well as theirs might be a cause for more reasoning. For the sake of peace there is no point in arguing over and over again about who is right or wrong. These are just different opinions which are true in view of each person's experience. Tolerance in this instance broadens your thinking ability.

When you cultivate greater tolerance in your life you grow in love, and you create greater balance and inner peace. It is always better to be honest and truthful and admit when you have made a mistake or when you are wrong rather than fighting your corner for the sake of pride.

Additionally, you will become more tolerant when you allow yourself to get to know people better. In most instances our relationships with others are superficial; we know them yet we hardly understand them. Strictly speaking, we know them but we do not know their values, their beliefs, their passions, what makes them tick, what turns them off, because we do not intend to know more about them by asking questions in order to create real rapport with them. Growing in tolerance means becoming a greater listener.

Tolerance is equal to love because when you choose to be more tolerant you always have love in mind.

"Tolerance is giving to every other human being every right that you claim for yourself."
– Robert Green Ingersoll

6. Deliverance through forgiveness

There is no greater way of finding inner peace than through forgiveness. This implies both to forgive yourself and forgive others. Countless are those who live this plane bitter as opposed to better. Bitter because they resented another or others all their life and thus lived a life of misery.

It is simply better to forgive and forget. It is not a question of forgiving and not forgetting but to forgive and forget. When you choose not to forget it is as if you have not forgiven at all.

♥ How do you forgive?

This is probably our biggest challenge as human beings because our ego (Edging God Out) gets in the way.

As in the excerpt from Matthew 5:43-45: "You have heard that it was said: 'You shall love your neighbour and hate your enemy.' But I say to you, love your enemies and pray for those who persecute you, so that you may be children of God." Pray for your enemy and you will experience miracles in your own life. Forgiving your enemies is a real test with regard to your capacity to love.

Mary Johnson's story is truly remarkable. She found forgiveness in her heart. She is the founder of the Minneapolis Support Group: 'From Death to Life.' She created the support group in memory of her son who was murdered back in the 1990's. Five years before the release of her son's killer she visited him in prison and she forgave him. In her own words she said: "The visit brought me to my knees. I knew that I knew that all of the anger, animosity and hatred I had felt for him was over with. It was gone! He is like my son."

She made the decision to live the rest of her life better as opposed to bitter. When you only live with love in your heart, miracles happen! As you progress in self-realization you will expand your capacity to love and forgive.

Exercise 13

Ho'oponopono is an ancient Hawaiian practice of reconciliation and forgiveness. You can practise Ho'oponopono cleaning process in your mind by repeating the following four sentences, which carry miraculous powers:

- ♥ I am sorry.
- ♥ Please forgive me.
- ♥ Thank-you!
- ♥ I love you.

"Forgiving love is compassion. You should understand that the state of forgiveness is much higher than that of spiritually nurturing others; it is a step closer to the state of God."
– Master Ryuho Okawa

Afterword

"Life is an opportunity, benefit from it.
Life is beauty, admire it.
Life is a dream, realize it.
Life is a challenge, meet it.
Life is a duty, complete it.
Life is a game, play it.
Life is a promise, fulfil it.
Life is sorrow, overcome it.
Life is a song, sing it.
Life is a struggle, accept it.
Life is a tragedy, confront it.
Life is an adventure, dare it.
Life is luck, make it.
Life is too precious, do not destroy it.
Life is life, fight for it."

– Mother Teresa

About the Author

Pascale Gibon otherwise known as the "Change Catalyst" is passionate about personal transformation and success. An avid reader she discovered her passion for writing in 2009.

She is a certified Jack Canfield Trainer in The Success Principles, a Licensed LifeSuccess Consultant, A Master Results Coach, and a Passion Test Facilitator. She has taught and facilitated personal development as an International Transformational and Success Trainer since 2009.

Pascale Gibon is also the founder of YES! To Training (Y.T.T – YES! to True Transformation), your self-empowerment portal for transformation which has been designed to help you bounce back, turn your life around and regain your zest for life.

YES! To Love Academy is the umbrella for her live events where she takes you through deep transformation through her various workshops.

She is the creator of the 3 M's Formula of Everyday Life Balance™, The Creative Process of Happiness™, and The Sand Paper Project.

As a visionary, intuitive and creative Pascale continues to work towards her life's purpose: inspiring and empowering women across the world to live happy, meaningful and miraculous lives.

Meet her at: https://www.pascalegibon.com

NOTES

NOTES

www.ingramcontent.com/pod-product-compliance
Lightning Source LLC
Chambersburg PA
CBHW060436090426
42733CB00011B/2300

* 9 7 8 0 9 9 3 5 1 9 8 0 2 *